South Arabia
Ancient to Islamic

Jeffrey V. Bailey

Table of Content

INTRODUCTION 6
CHAPTER I. HISTORICAL OVERVIEW OF 6th CENTURY SOUTH ARABIA 15
1. POLITICAL SITUATION 16
1.1 POLITICAL HISTORY BEFORE 6TH CENTURY AND SOUTH ARABIAN KINGDOMS16
1.1.1. The Kingdom of Saba' 17
1.1.2. The Minaean kingdom 19
1.1.3. Qatabān 21
1.1.4. Ḥaḍramawt 22
1.1.5. Ḥimyar 24
1.1.6. Kinda 26
1.2. THE POLITICAL SITUATION IN THE 6TH CENTURY CE 28
1.3. THE DECLINE OF SOUTH ARABIA 30
2. ECONOMY AND SOCIAL ORGANIZATION 32
2.1. ECONOMIC DEVELOPMENT 32
2.2. SOUTH ARABIAN COINAGE 34
.... 34
2.3. SOCIAL ORGANIZATION 35
3. CULTURE AND RELIGION 38
3.1. ANCIENT SOUTH ARABIAN LANGUAGES 38
3.1.1. Sabaic 39
3.1.2. Minaic (Madhābic) 40
3.1.3. Qatabānian 41
3.1.4. Ḥaḍramitic 41
3.2 RELIGION IN SOUTH ARABIA 42
3.2.1 Polytheism 42
3.2.2. Conversion to monotheism 43
3.2.3 Judaism 45
3.2.4. Christianity 47
CHAPTER II. ANALYSIS OF HISTORICAL SOURCES 48
1. ANCIENT SOUTH ARABIAN INSCRIPTIONS 48
1.1. al-Ašʿar (*ʾs²ʿrⁿ*) 49
1.3. ʿAkk (*ʿkᵐ*) 50
1.4. Ǧarm (*grm*) 51

1.5. Hamdān (*hmdn*) 52
1.6. Ḫawlan (*ḫwln*) 53
1.7. Ḥimyar (*ḥmyr*^{m}) 60
1.8. Kinda (*kdt*) 66
1.11. Murād 70
2. MEDIEVAL HISTORICAL SOURCES 71
2.1. HISTORY 71
2.1.1 al-ʾAšʿar 73
2.1.2 ʿAkk 73
2.1.3 Ğarm 74
2.1.4. Hamdān 75
2.1.5 Ḫawlān 76
2.1.6. Ḥimyar 76
2.1.7. Kinda 77
2.1.8. Maḏḥiğ 78
2.1.9. Mahra 79
2.2. THE AFTERMATH OF THE WARS OF APOSTASY 80

INTRODUCTION

In the period prior to the arrival of Islam, South Arabia was populated by tribes which were an ethnic and linguistic group distinct from the Arabs. The history of these tribes included periods of integration and fragmentation, the political status of the tribes underwent changes, and their relations were dynamic. The period which preceded Islamization was characterized by significant changes: the transition from polytheism to monotheism, political fragmentation, loss of political independence and conquest first by Ethiopia, then by the Sassanid Empire, economic decline and depopulation. After South Arabian tribes became part of the Islamic caliphate, they were almost completely Arabized and lost their identity as a distinct civilization.

The purpose of this thesis is to analyze the political and cultural changes, which these tribes experienced as a result of Islamization. The key period covers the 6th and 7th centuries CE, through the so-called Wars of the Apostasy i.e. Ridda wars, with relevant information regarding earlier centuries analyzed for comparative purposes. Research is based on the reconstruction of information on individual tribes by analysis of pre-Islamic inscriptions, which is compared with information from medieval Islamic historiography in order to analyze the changes that have occurred regarding the political situation of the tribes and in their relationships with one another.

Literature review

In order to study this topic, various aspects of the history of South Arabia in the period from the 2nd century BCE until the Ridda Wars are analyzed. The period between 2nd and 3rd century CE had particular importance for understanding the history of South Arabia as a period of significant political transformation. Also the period between 6th and 7th century CE can be considered as a turning point. During the 6th century CE, South Arabia experienced a period of political crisis, growth of influence of various states, changing relations between the

South Arabian tribes and tribal conflicts, whereas the 7th century CE is directly connected with the adoption of Islam and the political consequences of Islamization.

Regarding the first period, which covers the 2nd and 3rd centuries BCE, the key book is "L'unification du Yémen antique: la lutte entre Saba, Himyar et le Hadramawt du 1er au IIIème siècle de l'ère chrétienne" written by Muḥammad ʿAbd al-Qādir Bāfaqīh[1]. In this study, the unification process of South Arabia and its political consequences are examined against the backdrop of the complex relationships of various political forces: the South Arabian tribes and their political structures, the nomadic tribes of Bedouin Arabs and other external forces. Regarding the purpose of this thesis, the most relevant is the second chapter «The forces in the field», in which the system of relations between tribes, as well as the specifics of their political organization, are reconstructed based on inscriptions and geographical information. An example of an analysis of the problem of an individual tribe is presented in Chapter 7, which sheds light on the origin and role of the Ḫawlān tribe, as well as their relationship with the Sabaean Kingdom.

While Bāfaqīh has built his research on the painstaking reconstruction of the chronology of events and their political analysis, Andrey Korotayev uses a different approach to conceptualizing material in his work "Pre-Islamic Yemen"[2], which is devoted to the same period. His research is based on a consistent analysis of the key elements of the socio-political structure: royal power, *qayls*[3], and clan relations. As a result, his analysis of the formation of ancient South Arabian socio-political system gives us an idea of the integration process in the 2nd and 3rd centuries BCE from the point of view of interaction at the level of the individual elements of the socio-political system.

The sixth century CE, which, as a turning point in the history of South Arabia, is characterized by significant changes in all spheres of society, was often an object of research. Interpretations and evaluations of researchers of this period diverge. On the one

---

1 Muḥammad 'Abd al-Qādir Bāfaqīh: L'unification du Yémen antique: la lutte entre Saba, Himyar et le Hadramawt du 1er au IIIème siècle de l'ère chrétienne. Paris: Librairie Orientalist Paul Geuthner, 1990 (Bibliotheque de Raydan, 1).

2 Andrey Korotayev: *Pre-Islamic Yemen.* Wiesbaden: Harrassowitz Verlag, 1996.

3

hand, it is viewed as a period of crisis and decline, as well as a turning point in the break with the past. On the other hand, it can be considered as a transitional form, and hence the source of continuity for the subsequent period. From the conceptual point of view, «À la veille de l'islam: effondrement ou transformation du monde antique?» by Jérémie Schiettecatte[4] is crucial. While it doesn't focus exclusively on South Arabia, it deals with Arabian Peninsula as a whole. Schiettecatte considers an important question of the approach to the analysis of this period preceding the adoption of Islam: is it a manifestation of rupture or continuity with the past?

In general, the number of studies of the history of the entire Arabian Peninsula in the period on the eve of Islam is increasing in recent times. There are a few early studies which are relevant to the issue of South Arabia in the 5th and 6th century CE, for example, "South Arabia in the 6th century" by Avraam Lundin, published in 1961[5]. Of course, this study is not devoid of the classical shortcomings of Soviet historiography, especially in the chapter "The Social System of Southern Arabia in the 6th Century". In addition to describing key foreign policy developments with an emphasis on the Ḥimyar-Ethiopian war, Lundin analyzes the transformation of the state structure as well as the political crises in the 6th century CE. However, the key factor in this study is royal power, so Lundin pays little attention to tribes and tribal relations.

The dissertation "South Arabia in the 5th and 6th centuries CE, with reference to relations with Central Arabia" by Khalid Salih Al-Asali[6], defended in 1968, offers an example of a comparative study. Firstly, this approach not only articulates the specifics of the political structure of the South Arabian tribes, but also shows which preconditions for a cultural and political transfer during the process of Islamization already existed in the

---

4 Jérémie Schiettecatte: "À la veille de l'"islam: effondrement ou transformation du monde antique." *Les préludes de l'islam. Ruptures et continuités des civilisations du Proche-Orient, de l'Afrique orientale, de l'Arabie et de l'Inde à la veille de l'Islam*. Éd. Christian Robin et Jérémie Schiettecatte. Paris: De Boccard, 2013 (Orient et Méditerranée, 11), pp. 9-36.

5 Avraam Lundin: *Juzhnaja Aravija v VI veke* [South Arabia in the 6th Century]. Moskva, Leningrad: Izdatel'stvo Akademii nauk SSSR, 1961 (Palestinskij sbornik 8(71)).

6 Khalid Salih Al-Asali: *South Arabia in the 5th and 6th centuries CE, with reference to relations* with Central Arabia. Ph.D. Diss., University of St. Andrews, 1968.

previous period. This thesis is also useful for clarifying the issues of ethnogenesis in this space and political relationships in this period.

A study by Mikhail Piotrovsky, "South Arabia in the Early Middle Ages"[7], covers a broader period from the 5th to the 10th century CE. Specificity of Piotrovsky's approach is that he carefully traces the changes in society on the eve of Islam and after Islamization by choosing a thematic focus. This study covers a wide range of topics: political history, the dynamics of the relationship between nomads and sedentary tribes, the social structure of society and religious issues. Piotrovsky doesn't consider the transformation which took place during the Islamization process as a radical break from the past; his goal is to analyze the degree of continuity between the social forms before and after the adoption of Islam. The choice of the timeframe of his research creates the concept of a single "early medieval epoch", and the study itself demonstrates "the unity of fundamental processes."

At a thematic level, studies devoted to Ancient South Arabia cover a wide range of issues: linguistic diversity and the problem of inscriptions, economic history, trade development, urbanization, issues of ethno-genesis and population dynamics, etc. Particular attention is paid to research related to religious practices and their transformation in South Arabia. Studies cover such topics as the transition from polytheism to monotheism, the problems of the spread of Christianity and Judaism. The majority of the studies which focus on religious issues also contribute to the study of political transformations in South Arabian society. The study of religious practices sheds light on the specifics of religious policy and its consequences, as well as on the political factors influencing, among others, the choice of religion at the state level.

For example, "Le royaume de Himyar à l'époque monothéiste" by Iwona Gajda[8] considers the conversion of monotheism as an instrument of political unification. Gajda begins her research by examining religious issues in a historical perspective and demonstrating how various historical events and political structure influenced religious

---

7 Mikhail Piotrovsky: *Juzhnaja Aravija v rannee srednevekov'e. Stanovlenie srednevekovogo obshhestva* [South Arabia in the Early Middle Ages. The Formation of a Medieval Society]. Moskva: Nauka, 1985.

8 Iwona Gajda: *Le royaume de Himyar à l'époque monothéiste.* Paris: De Boccard, 2009 (Mémoires de l'Académie des inscriptions et belles-lettres, 40).

practices. Gajda pays a lot of attention to the problem of diversity (ethnic, linguistic, religious) and its influence on the formation of the social and political structure of the kingdom Ḥimyar. Analyzing the implications of the conversion to monotheism in the policies of the Ḥimyarite kingdom, Gajda demonstrates its consolidating effect on the social and tribal structure of the South Arabian society. From the point of view of the transformation of the political status of tribes, this study clarifies how monotheistic religious practices influenced the tribal organization and the distribution of power between tribes.

This focus is also characteristic for studies of religious practices of individual tribes. The main research concerns the tribe of Kinda. Christian Robin in "Les religions pratiquées par les membres de la tribu de Kinda (Arabie) à la veille de l'Islam"[9] reconstructs the main events related to the religious self-determination of this tribe. This study also examines religious practices of different social strata within the tribe. The main issue relates to the study of the problem of conversion to Judaism and its role in the political history of the tribe. A similar question, but in a later period, is analyzed by Michael Lecker in his article "Judaism among Kinda and the ridda of Kinda"[10]. In this case, the issue of the spread of Judaism among Kindite tribal members is considered within the context of their resistance to the caliphate and the consequences of this resistance.

Studies of the persecution of Christians are also important for understanding the political processes of that period. Norbert Nebes in the article "Die Märtyrer von Nagrān und das Ende der Ḥimyar. Zur politischen Geschichte Südarabiens im frühen sechsten Jahrhundert"[11] investigates the persecution of Christians in Nagrān, and analyzed these events in the context of the political situation and religious policy of Ḥimyarite Kingdom. The article «Nagrān vers l'époque du massacre: notes sur l'histoire politique, économique et

---

9 Christian Robin: "Les religions pratiquées par les membres de la tribu de Kinda (Arabie) à la veille de l'Islam," *Judaïsm ancien - Ancient Judaism*, 1 (2013), pp.203-261.

10 Michael Lecker: "Judaism among Kinda and the Ridda of Kinda," *Journal of the American Oriental Society*, Vol. 115, No. 4 (1995), pp. 635-650.

11 Norbert Nebes: "Die Märtyrer von Nagrān und das Ende der Ḥimyar. Zur politischen Geschichte Südarabiens im frühen sechsten Jahrhundert." *Aethiopica*, 11 (2021), pp. 7-40.

institutionnelle et sur l'introduction du christianisme» by Christian Robin[12] uses a similar approach, but in a broader perspective.

There are numerous studies which are thematically focused exclusively on political processes as well. Key to this topic is the thesis and a subsequent book based on it "Yemeni relations with the central Islamic authorities: (9-233/630-847); a political history" by Al-Medej[13]. The timeframe of the study covers the period from 630 to 847 CE, but their analysis is preceded by an extensive chapter devoted to the study of the previous era. Al-Medej pays attention to such issues as the political situation and its development, the distribution of power and inter-tribal relations as well. The first chapter also includes information on the first contacts of the South Arabian tribes with Islam. In the following chapters, Al-Medej carefully analyzes the role of the Yemeni tribes in military operations and their participation in movements, the dynamics of their resistance and cooperation in different territories. However, the pre-Islamic period in this study is presented only in an introductory context.

Generally speaking, studies of political processes in South Arabia are characterized by an approach in which the key factor is the royal authority; for instance, the works by Jacques Ryckmans "L'Institution monarchique en Arabie méridionale avant l'Islam: Ma'în et Saba"[14] and A.F.L. Beeston "Kingship in Ancient South Arabia"[15] focus on the state structure and the analysis of terms and concepts associated with the higher layers of power. A number of studies are devoted to the political history of individual kingdoms and is based on the re-creation of events on the basis of pre-Islamic inscriptions (for example, François Bron

---

12 Christian Robin: "Nagrān vers l'époque du massacre: notes sur l'histoire politique, économique et institutionnelle et sur l'introduction du christianisme." *Juifs et chrétiens en Arabie aux Ve et VIe siècles: regards croisés sur les sources.* Éd. J. Beaucamp, F. Briquel-Chatonnet et Ch.Robin. Paris: ACHCByz, 2010 (Monographies 32 - Le massacre de Nagrān II), pp. 39-106.

13 A A M M M Al-Medej: Yemeni relations with the central Islamic authorities: (9-233/630-847); a political history. Ph.D. Diss., Durham University, 1983.

14 Jacques Ryckmans: *L'Institution monarchique en Arabie méridionale avant l'Islam: Ma'în et Saba.* Louvain: Publications universitaires, 1951.

15 A.F.L. Beeston: "Kingship in Ancient South Arabia." *Journal of the Economic and Social History of the Orient*, Vol. 15, No. 3 (1972), pp. 256-268.

"La crise du royaume de Saba' au IIème siècle de notre ère"[16]; Christian Robin "Le royaume hujride, dit «royaume de Kinda», entre Himyar et Byzance"[17] and "Before Himyar: Epigraphic Evidence for the Kingdoms of South Arabia"[18], as well as in "Le Royaume Sud-Arabe de Qatabân et sa Datation" by Jacqueline Pirenne[19]).

Andrey Korotayev analyzes the transformation of the socio-political structure and state entities through the concepts of "state" - "chiefdom" - "tribe" in his numerous articles and a book "Social History of Yemen"[20]. Through the use of these concepts, he identifies the factors that have influenced political transformation, and also builds a general scheme for the evolution of South Arabian society. From the point of view of the study of the transformation of the political status of tribes, a part of the study is devoted to the genesis of the tribal structure.

To analyze the tribal structure, tribal relations, as well as the specific features of individual tribal formations, numerous articles by Robin are useful. In the article "Esquisse d'une histoire de l'organisation tribale en Arabie du Sud antique"[21] he explores the structure of tribes, their emergence and transformation. Starting with his dissertation "Le pays de Ḥamdān et Ḥawlān Qudāʿat (Nord-Yemen), avant l'Islam"[22], Robin examines the problem of tribal confederations, the methods of tribal genesis and the relationship between a clan and a tribe (for example, also in his works "Le problème de Hamdān: des qayls aux trois tribus"[23]

16 François Bron: "La crise du royaume de Saba' au II ème siècle de notre ère," *Orientalia* NOVA SERIES, Vol. 71, No. 4 (2002), pp. 417-423.

17 Christian Robin: "Le royaume hujride, dit « royaume de Kinda », entre Himyar et Byzance," *Comptes rendus des séances de l'Académie des Inscriptions et Belles-Lettres*, Vol. 140, N. 2 (1996), pp. 665-714.

18 Christian Robin: "Before Himyar: Epigraphic Evidence for the Kingdoms of South Arabia." *Arabs and Empires before Islam*. Ed. Greg Fisher. New York: Oxford University Press, 2015, pp. 90-127.

19 Jacqueline Pirenne: *Le royaume sud-arabe de Qataban et sa datation: d'apres l'archeologie et les sources classiques jusqu'au Periple de la Mer Erythree.* Louvain: Publications universitaires, 1961.

20 Andrey Korotayev: *Social'naja istorija Jemena, X v. do n.e. - XX v. n.e. Vozhdestva i plemena strany Hashid i Bakil* [Social History of Yemen, X century. BCE - XX century CE. The Chiefdoms and Tribes of the Country Hashid and Bakil]. Moskva: URSS, 2006.

21 Christian Robin: "Esquisse d'une histoire de l'organisation tribale en Arabie du Sud antique." *La péninsule Arabique d'aujourd'hui.* T. II. *Etudes par pays.* Éd. P. Bonnenfant. Aix-en-Provence: Institut de recherches et d'études sur le monde arabe et musulman, 1982, pp. 17–30.

22 Christian Robin: Le pays de Ḥamdān et Ḥawlān Qudāʿat (Nord-Yemen), avant l'Islam. Diss., Paris, 1977.

23 Christian Robin: "Le problème de Hamdān: des qayls aux trois tribus. " *Proceedings of the Seminar for Arabian Studies,* Vol. 8 (1978), pp. 46-52.

and "Saba' et la Khawlān du Nord (Khawlān Gudādān): l'organisation et la gestion des conquêtes par les royaumes d'Arabie méridionale"[24]).

Another example of a study of the specifics of formations of tribes and their unions is the thesis by Mahfouz Said al-Zahrani titled "L'histoire des tribus Kinda et Madhhij en Arabie preislamique, des origines jusqu'au VI' siecle de l'ere chretienne"[25]. As far as complex tribal genesis is concerned, this thesis is interesting for the detailed reconstruction of tribal organization. Particular emphasis in this study is given to the analysis of the social and political role of both tribes in general, as well as individual tribes within the confederation, as well as individual clans.

Since most studies focus on general political history or on individual tribes, there is a gap in research at the intermediate level, that is, the systematic study of tribes of different significance and their complex relationships. On the other hand, with rare exceptions, most studies concentrate either on the period before or the period after Islamization. This thesis aims to investigate the transitional period and trace the changes brought about by Islamization as a political factor.

The purpose of this thesis is to analyze how the political situation of South Arabian tribes changed during the adoption of Islam. The main goal behind my thesis is to compare the sources regarding ancient South Arabian tribes. These tribes existed before Islam, and the purpose of this thesis is to see how their political, cultural and national nature and structure changed during the process of Islamisation and Arabisation.

For this purpose, thesis is methodologically based on a comparative analysis of tribal organization and distribution of power between tribes. This comparative analysis includes the juxtaposition of historical sources, both the pre-Islamic South Arabian inscriptions as well as the later Islamic medieval sources.

---

24 Christian Robin: "Saba' et la Khawlān du Nord (Khawlān Gudādān): l'organisation et la gestion des conquêtes par les royaumes d'Arabie méridionale." *Issledovanija po Aravii i islamu. Sbornik statej b čect' 70-letija Muhaila Borisoviča Piotrovskogo* [Studies on Arabia and Islam. A collection of papers in honour of Mikhail Borishovich Piotrovskij on the occasion of his 70th birthday]. Ed. Alexander V. Sedov. Moskva: Gosudarstvennyj Muzej Vostoka, 2014, pp. 156-203.

25 Mahfouz Said Al-Zahrani: L'histoire des tribus Kinda et Madhhij en Arabie preislamique, des origines jusqu'au VIe siecle de l'ere chretienne. Thesis, Aix-en-Provence: Université de Provence, 2000.

Thus, the basis of the thesis is based on two types of sources.

1. Pre-Islamic inscriptions. The primary sources of information about the pre-Islamic South Arabian history are monumental inscriptions which were written in a South Arabian script called *musnad*, which also means "inscription" in all of the Ancient South Arabian languages[26].They are very formulaic and usually report only dedications to deities, the construction of public buildings, military campaigns and law codes. They almost never allude to any events outside of the South Arabian area, which often makes it difficult to determine the correct date of a given inscription[27]. These pre-Islamic inscriptions can be found on the DASI website (http://dasi.humnet.unipi.it/index.php?id=42&prjId=1&corId=0&colId=0). The ASA (Ancient South Arabian) corpus is one of the most interesting collections of epigraphic documents of the Semitic world, first and foremost for its vastness. With over 15,000 inscriptions, it is the fullest epigraphic corpus of the culture that flourished in South Arabia from the late second millennium BC to the sixth century AD.

2. Medieval Islamic historiography written in Arabic. Primarily the accounts of the Ridda wars written by the later Muslim historians, specifically aṭ-Ṭabari. This type of historical source can be used not only to obtain information about subsequent events, but also to refine and supplement the information found in pre-Islamic inscriptions.

Thesis Structure

The first chapter will give an overview of the political, cultural, religious and linguistic situation in the South Arabian region in the period prior to the conversion of the region to Islam. The chapter will focus on the 6th century CE onward, with a very brief

---

26 Maraqten 1998, pp. 287

27 Robert G. Hoyland: *Arabia and the Arabs, From the Bronze Age to the Coming of Islam*. New York: Routledge, 2001. P. 36.

summary of some relevant information regarding the previous centuries. Also the factors which led to decline of South Arabia will be analyzed. The second part of this chapetr deals with such question as social structure and economic history, languages and their specifics, conversion to monotheism, the role of Judaism and Christianity in the region.

The second and main chapter will compare both the ancient inscriptions as well as in the medieval historical sources and analyze which tribes are mentioned in both sources. The chapter will be divided into two parts. The first one will focus on the ancient inscriptions. Based on these materials, references to each tribe and tribal alliances will be analyzed from theory point of view of political history and their political status. The second part will examine how these tribes are described in the medieval Islamic sources for the Ridda wars and what role they played in these events. Ultimately, through the comparison of these two sources, the political changes these tribes underwent between the pre-Islamic era and the period when the region became part of the nascent Caliphate will be made clearer.

CHAPTER I. HISTORICAL OVERVIEW OF 6th CENTURY SOUTH ARABIA

South Arabia experienced a turbulent period in the 6th century CE, not only politically but also culturally. The first chapter is devoted to a general overview of situation and historical development of pre-Islamic South Arabia, as well as the situation on the eve of the so-called Wars of Apostasy. This chapter will focus on pre-Islamic South Arabia from the 6th century CE onward, with a brief overview of relevant information regarding earlier centuries.

The South Arabian region is notable for its cultural and political heterogeneity, and its history was marked by many state entities, tribes, tribal unions and other political actors. The first part of this chapter analyzes the main South Arabian kingdoms and their relationship with each other. The main focus is the overview of the events of the 6th century CE, when the region faced both a domestic political crisis and foreign policy problems that led to the conquest of South Arabia first by Ethiopia, then by the Sassanid Empire. Special attention is given to the political, economic and demographic factors that led to the decline of the region.

The second part of this chapter is devoted to the socio-economic and cultural characteristics of the region. The chapter contains a brief historical overview of the region's economic development and an analysis of the social structure of South Arabian tribes and states. The chapter also deals with the issues of linguistic heterogeneity and the characteristics of ancient South Arabian languages. The last section is devoted to the issue of religious transformation and religious policy. South Arabia experienced a transition from polytheism to monotheism in this period, the formation of which was influenced by Judaism and Christianity. The role which Judaism and Christianity played in the history of the region is analyzed as well.

1. POLITICAL SITUATION

The political situation in South Arabia before the adoption of Islam can be described as alternating periods of political unification and fragmentation. At the same time, the fragmentation and the resulting political conflicts far outweigh the periods of political unity. One of the factors that influenced such political dynamics is the geography of the region. The rugged terrain and the combination of different geographic regions created a natural obstacle for effective political unification. On the other hand, cultural and ethnographic heterogeneity lead to internal political conflicts between tiribes, as well as between state power and nobility. These conflicts complicated political centralization.

This subchapter looks at the brief history of state entities that existed in South Arabia before the 6th century CE, as well as the processes of unification and conquest that took place between them. In addition, the influence of external factors on the development of the foreign policy situation will be analyzed in the subchapter. Among these factors are the relationship with nomadic tribes coming from the north, the influence and interference of neighboring states, as well as influential countries in world politics. Armed conflicts with neighboring states eventually led to the loss of state independence. The last part of the subchapter analyzes this process, as well as the accompanying political crisis and fragmentation. In addition to political factors, in the part of the subchapter on the decline of South Arabia, other factors that lead to this decline will be analyzed.

1.1 POLITICAL HISTORY BEFORE 6TH CENTURY AND SOUTH ARABIAN KINGDOMS

In this subchapter, a brief overview of the history of the major ancient South Arabian kingdoms until the 6th century CE will be given. In addition to the history of the kingdoms, the subchapter briefly examines the relationship between them. For each kingdom, facts such as the formation and evolution of the political structure, religious and linguistic characteristics, brief information about economic development, as well as the decline of the kingdom are analyzed.

1.1.1. The Kingdom of Saba'

The period of Sabaean domination extended from the 8th century BCE to the 3rdcentury CE, when Ḥimyar became the dominant political force in South Arabia. The Sabaean kingdom culturally dominated the region, and it was, as Robin notes "a model in a number of fields": for example, among other things, the Sabaean language and dating system spread far beyond the borders of the kingdom itself[28].

The Sabaeans, like the other south Arabian peoples, were unified by their worship of the god 'Almaqah. The unifying effect was the figure of the deity itself, which was strengthened by the performance of general religious rituals and festivities[29].

---

28 Robin: "Before Himyar," p. 95.
29 Hoyland: *Arabia and the Arabs,* p.36.

In the initial period, an important role in public administration was played by *mukarribs*. They performed not only sacred, economic and organizational functions, but political and administrative functions as well[30]. According to Korotayev, during this period, the kingdom is characterized by a developed state apparatus and a high level of political centralization[31].

The basis of the economy was agriculture developed irrigation system, which was built and supported by the efforts of the state apparatus[32]. Caravan trade also played an important role: although Sabeans did not produce aromatics, they aspired to control trade routes[33]. Due to the economic and environmental crisis caused by the difficulties in the operation of irrigation systems, by the end of the 1st millennium BCE the kingdom of Saba᾿ is in a state of decline[34]. However, by the turn of the millennium the kingdom experienced a period of stabilization, both in political and economic spheres[35].

Due to military campaigns, Sabaeans managed to expand the territory of their state, adding neighboring territories and thereby spreading their cultural influence[36]. Military conflicts occurred often, while the military actions of the kingdom were mainly conducted in foreign territories, and mostly, the Sabaean kingdom had to fight simultaneously on several fronts[37].

The Sabaeans managed to extend their dominance in this way over other states in the region, such as Ḥaḍramawt, Qatabān and Maʿīn[38]. It was at the end of the 3rd century A.D. that the political unification of ancient Yemen was achieved with Saba' and Ḏū Raydān united

---

30 Avraam Lundin: *Gosudarstvo mukarribov Saba : sabejskij eponimat* [The State of Mukarribs - Saba: Sabean eponymat]. Moskva: Nauka, 171. P. 182.

31 Korotayev: *Social'naja istorija Jemena,* p. 83.

32 *Ibid.*

33 A.F.L. Beeston: "The Arabian Aromatics Trade in Antiquity," *Proceedings of the Seminar for Arabian Studies*, 2005, p. 58.

34 Pirenne, Jacqueline: Paléographie des inscriptions sud-arabes. Contribution à la chronologie et à l'histoire de l'Arabie du Sud antique, Tome I: Des origines jusqu'à l'époque himyarite. Bruxelles: Paleis der Academiën, 1956. P. 175-178.

35 Korotayev: *Social'naja istorija Jemena,* p. 101.

36 Hoyland: *Arabia and the Arabs,* p. 47.

37 Bāfaqīh: *L'unification du Yémen antique*, p. 140.

38 Al-Medej: *Yemeni relations*, p.7.

under the rule of the Banū Ḏū Raydān [39]. Thus, a political unification of South Arabia under one ruler was accomplished.

As a result, in the kingdom a political system was formed, which can be characterized as federation or confederation. Korotaev claims that the state structure of the Sabaean kingdom in this period can be characterized as a combination of weak central state power with chiefdoms on the periphery[40]. According to his analysis, the role in consolidating the territory was played not so much by vertical centralization as by horizontal networks[41]. Such networks included religious, ancestral and clan relations.

This state formation with a weak degree of political centralization experienced problems with the functioning of state mechanisms, which led to decentralization and political crisis. The crisis was deepened by the struggle for power of representatives of different dynasties and noble families[42].

The crisis was also caused by the raids of nomadic tribes, which not only created a constant threat to the northern borders, but attacked caravans as well[43]. The economic crisis associated with the decline of trade routes also influenced the decline of the kingdom.

This difficult situation was exploited by the kingdom of Ḥimyar, which captured part of Sabaean territory. During this period, the kingdom of Saba' tried to find allies by uniting with Ḥaḍramawt or Ethiopia[44]. As a result, the Sabaeans managed to halt the expansion of Ḥimyar for some time and regain control of their territories. However, as a result of all crisis factors, Ḥimyar finally conquered the Sabaean kingdom by the end of the 3rd century CE and

39 Bāfaqīh: *L'unification du Yémen antique*, p. 319.
40 Korotayev: *Social'naja istorija Jemena,* p. 82.
41 Ibid., p. 102.
42 Bron: "La crise du royaume de Saba'," 418.
43 On the other hand, the nomadic tribes influenced the genesis of the tribal organization: Christian Robin: "La pénétration des Arabes nomades au Yémen." *Revue du monde musulman et de la Méditerranée*, Vol. 61, N. 1 (1991), pp. 71-88.
44 Bāfaqīh: *L'unification du Yémen antique*, p. 411.

Saba' lost its political independence[45]. The Sabaean culture retained its influence however (for example, in the terms of language and royal titles)[46].

1.1.2. The Minaean kingdom

The earliest evidence relating to the Minaeans dated from the 8th to 7th centuries BCE[47]. The flowering of the kingdom took place in the period between the 4th and the 2nd century BCE, and it ceased to exist in the 1st century BCE[48]. Its territory was concentrated primarily in the Wādī Madhāb in the Yemeni Jawf. In fact, its territory was an enclave among the Sabaean possessions[49].

A distinctive feature of the Minaean kingdom was peaceful character of their policy. The Minean kingdom was the only one among the four pre-Ḥimyarite South Arabian kingdoms who had no territorial aspirations and did not conduct military campaigns[50]. Unlike the other South Arabian political entities, they also did not participate in the formation of tribal unions[51].

The way of life of the Minaeans was sedentary[52]. Their own territory was small, but the network of trade ties established by them was extremely wide. The key to the economy of the Minaean kingdom was trade, which was also a tool to spread their influence[53]. They managed to take over the control of the caravan trade from the Sabaeans, who had previously

---

45 Hoyland: *Arabia and the Arabs,* p. 60.

46 Christian Robin: "Les langues de la Péninsule Arabique," *Revue du monde musulman et de la Méditerranée,* Vol. 61, N. 1 (1991), pp. 95-97.

47 Mounir Arbach and Irene Rossi: "From city-state to kingdom: history and chronology of Maʿīn between the VIII and the VI centuries BCE," *Orientalia,* 81/4 (2012), pp. 322.

48 Hoyland: *Arabia and the Arabs,* p. 40.

49 Christian Robin: "Quelques épisodes marquants de l'histoire sudarabique." *Revue du monde musulman et de la Méditerranée,* Vol. 61, N. 1 (1991), p. 58.

50 Hoyland: *Arabia and the Arabs,* p. 41.

51 Beeston: "Kingship in Ancient South Arabia," p. 257.

52 Robin: "Quelques épisodes marquants," p.58.

53 Beeston: "The Arabian Aromatics Trade in Antiquity," p. 60-61.

held monopoly on aromatic trade, in the 6th century BCE[54], which is the century in which the Minaean kingdom seems to have increased in influence.

The Minaeans had their own language, which was an adapted version of the language that existed earlier in the Wādī Madhāb[55], and which spread beyond the the territory of their kingdom due to their trading activities[56]. In addition to their language, the Minaeans had their own religious pantheon and a specific political and social structure.

The power of the king was limited, and the royal advisors had wide authority. Many of the functions which were the prerogative of the state administration in other kingdoms (for example, construction of temples and irrigation systems), were under the control of aristocratic clans in the Minaean kingdom[57]. Due to these facts, the Minaean kingdom is described by researchers as a"merchant republic'.[58]

In the 2nd and 1st century BCE the Minaean Kingdom faced an economic crisis similar to what the Sabaean kingdom had experienced during this period. However, the damage from the decline of caravan routes was harder for the Minaean Kingdom, since their economy was based on trade[59]. As a result, the kingdom lasted until ca. 120 BCE; when the kingdom became a vassal of Saba '[60].

1.1.3. Qatabān

Kingdom Qatabān, which arose at the turn of the 1st millennium BCE, existed until ca. 175 CE, when its territory was divided between the kingdoms of Saba' and Ḥaḍramawtt[61].

---

54 Robin: "Before Himyar," p.96.

55 Robin: " Les langues de la Péninsule Arabique," p. 98.

56 Leonid Kogan and Andrey Korotayev: "Sayhadic Languages (Epigraphic South Arabian). " *Semitic Languages*. Ed. Robert Hetzron. London: Routledge, 1997, p. 220.

57 Robin: "Before Himyar," p.96.

58 Ibid.

59 Robin: "Quelques épisodes marquants," pp. 62-63.

60 Robin: " Les langues de la Péninsule Arabique," p. 98.

61 Robin: " Les langues de la Péninsule Arabique," p. 98.

Qatabān was first mentioned as an ally of the kingdom of Saba in the inscription RES 3945 which commemorates the military campaigns of Karib''il Watar son of Ḏamar 'ali [62].

Agriculture based on the system of artificial irrigation formed the basis of the economy of the kingdom. The main element of economic activity was the economy of temples, which were under state control. In particular, part of the temple tithe was used in the public interest, thus becoming a form of taxation[63]. Qatabān also participated in the export and transport aromatics[64]. The regional significance of the kingdom was determined by the fact that trade routes linking other South Arabian kingdoms passed through its capital, the city of Timna.

The main deity, whose cult had a unifying effect, was 'Amm. They used the *musnad* script for their inscriptions, but their language was different from the Sabaean language[65]. The main distribution area of their language was Wādī Bayhān and Wādī Ḥārib, on the edge of the inner Ṣayhad desert[66],

Politically, the king's power relied heavily on noble families and landowners. Their assembly had some legislative power, and the king had to obey their decisions[67]. The role of noble families in the political system was also reinforced by the system of succession to the throne, which included the transfer of the throne to the son of some noble person, the first born after the election of the king[68]. Qatabān struggled for power in the region and regularly participated in armed conflicts with the kingdoms of Awsān, Ma'īn, Saba' and Ḥaḍramawt [69].

Due to its irrigation system and the successful adaptation of trade to activity to the changed conditions, the flowering of Qatabān occurred in the 2nd century BC[E70]. By the 3rd

62 Hoyland: *Arabia and the Arabs,* p. 42.

63 Korotayev: *Social'naja istorija Jemena,* p. 40.

64 Beeston: "The Arabian Aromatics Trade in Antiquity," p. 59.

65 Robin: " Les langues de la Péninsule Arabique," p. 98.

66 Kogan and Korotayev: "Sayhadic Languages, " p. 221.

67 Andrey Korotayev: "A socio-political conflict in the Qatabanian kingdom? (A preliminary re-interpretation of the Qatabanic inscription RÉS 3566)," *Proceedings of the Seminar for Arabian Studies,* Vol. 27 (1997), p. 143.

68 Avraam Lundin: "Prestolonasledie v Katabane" [Succession in Qatabān]. *Sovetskaja etnografija,* 4 (1978), pp. 123-130.

69 Hoyland: *Arabia and the Arabs,* p. 42.

70 Korotayev: *Social'naja istorija Jemena,* p. 103.

century BCE, Qatabān became strong enough to challenge Sabaean supremacy, which is attested by the fact than numerous inscriptions written in Qatabānian language have been discovered in areas previously under Sabaean control[71]. Victims of the expansionist policy of Qatabān became the kingdoms of Awsān.

As a result of the political crisis, the kingdom disintegrated and its territory was divided between the other kingdoms[72]. Firstly, Qatabān was attacked by the Ḥimyarite kingdom, but later taking advantage of the fact that Ḥimyar faced the united resistance of the kingdoms of Saba᾽ and Ḥaḍramawt, Qatabān experienced a short period of independence. Despite this, in finally Qatabān was conquered by Ḥaḍramawt and lost its political independence[73].

1.1.4. Ḥaḍramawt

The Kingdom of Ḥaḍramawt arose around the same time as Qatabān: at the turn of the 1st millennium BCE[74]. The capital of Ḥaḍramawt was the city of Šabwa, and its territory covered wadi Ḥaḍramawt and some adjoining areas.

Trade was of great importance to the kingdom of Ḥaḍramawtt[75]. The cultivation of frankincense groves and the production of aromatics were under state control. It was the first South Arabian kingdom which established ports (at modern-day Bīr ʿalī, was founded ca. the 1st century BCE, and Khōr Rōrī, which was founded ca. the 1st century BCE and was founded to ship aromatics from Ḏofār to the western part of South Arabia) in order to

---

71 Hoyland: *Arabia and the Arabs,* p. 42.
72 Robin: " Les langues de la Péninsule Arabique," p. 98.
73 Hoyland: *Arabia and the Arabs,* p. 47.
74 Ibid., 42.
75 Alexander Sedov: "Sea-trade of the Hadramawt Kingdom from the 1st to the 6th Centuries A.D." *Profumi d'Arabia. Atti del convegno.* A cura di A.Avanzini. Roma: L'Erma di Bretschneider, 1997 (Saggi di storia antica, 11), pp. 365-385.

participate in the maritime frankincense trade between India and the Mediterranean[76]. However, active trade exchange affected mainly the coast region rather than the hinterland [77].

During the crisis of the Sabaean kingdom in the 1st century BCE, the power of Ḥaḍramawt increased, especially the control over trade[78]. By the 1st century CE Ḥaḍramawt controlled most of the coast. Their period of prosperity extended from the 4th to the 2nd century BCE.

Ḥaḍramawt actively participated in the political struggle and conflicts between other South Arabian kingdoms: it fought against Qatabān and Ḥimyar and cooperated with Ma'in[79]. The dynamics of the relationship between the Sabaean kingdom and Ḥaḍramawt included different phases of confrontation or alliance[80]. On the one hand, Ḥaḍramawt experienced a strong cultural influence of the Sabaean kingdom, including in its socio-political structure[81]. Ḥaḍramawt acted as an ally of Saba against the Ḥimyarite kingdom in the 2nd century CE[82]. However the capital of Ḥaḍramawt was plundered in the confrontation with the Sabaean kingdom in the beginning of the 3rd century[83]. In the end, the struggle against Ḥimyarites was unsuccessful and in the 4th century Ḥaḍramawt was included in the Ḥimyarite kingdom[84]. There was, however, a series of revolts in the Ḥaḍramawt region in the early 4th century CE which Ḥimyar suppressed[85].

A detailed study of the kingdom of Ḥaḍramawt is difficult due to a small number of inscriptions. The Ḥaḍramitic language seems to have been the most divergent of all

---

76 Hoyland: *Arabia and the Arabs,* p. 43.

77 Sedov: "Sea-trade of the Hadramawt Kingdom," p. 372.

78 Ibid., p. 367.

79 Sergej Francuzov: *Istorija Hadramauta s drevnejshih vremen do konca britanskogo vladychestva. Tom 1. Istorija Hadramauta v epohu drevnosti* [History of Hadramaut from ancient times to the end of British rule. Volume 1. History of Hadramaut in the Age of Antiquity]. Sankt-Peterburg: Peterburgskoe lingvisticheskoe obshhestvo, 2014 (Studia Yemenica), p. 172.

80 Hoyland: *Arabia and the Arabs,* p. 44.

81 Francuzov: *Istorija Hadramauta v epohu drevnosti,* p. 71.

82 Bāfaqīh: *L'unification du Yémen antique*, p. 407.

83 Francuzov: *Istorija Hadramauta v epohu drevnosti,* p. 223.

84 Robin: "Quelques épisodes marquants," p. 63.

85 Hoyland: *Arabia and the Arabs,* p. 47.

South Arabian languages[86]. The head deity in the pantheon of Ḥaḍramawt was Sayyin (S'yn), in whose honor ritual celebrations and pilgrimages were held[87].

1.1.5. Ḥimyar

The Kingdom of Ḥimyar originated in the late 2nd century BCE[88]. The kingdom originally covered the territory in the area around capital city Ẓafār in the southern Yemeni highlands. In the early 1st century BCE Ḥimyar established control over the points of sea trade and a significant territory of the kingdom of Saba', even managing to capture the Sabaean capital Ma'rib for some time[89]. Ḥimyar also managed to seize part of the state of Qatabān, which as a result lost its political independence for the first time[90].

However, by the end of the 2nd century the kingdom of Ḥimyar faced a unified resistance. As a result of cooperation of the kingdoms of Saba' and Ḥaḍramawtt[91], with the participation of Ethiopian troops, it was possible to defeat the Ḥimyarite kingdom, so that Ḥimyar became dependent on the kingdom of Saba'[92].

The Ḥimyarites managed to quickly recover from this defeat by the end of the 3rd century (about 280), when they defeated and put an end to the political independence of the Sabaean kingdom[93]. A few decades later, the Ḥimyarites seized Ḥaḍramawt and incorporated it into their territory[94]. Thus, the Ḥimyarites also succeeded in ousting Ethiopians from the peninsula. Ḥimyarite kings took the long title "The King of Saba, ḏū-Raydān, Ḥaḍramawt and Yamnat"[95].

---

86 Robin: " Les langues de la Péninsule Arabique," p. 99.
87 Francuzov: *Istorija Hadramauta v epohu drevnosti,* pp. 143- 171.
88 Christian Robin: "Aux Origines de l'État Himyarite: Ḥimyar et Dhu-Raydan." *Arabian Studies in Honour of Mahmoud Ghul.* Wiesbaden: Harrassowitz Verlag, 1989, pp. 105.
89 Hoyland: *Arabia and the Arabs,* p. 47.
90 *Ibid.*
91 Francuzov: *Istorija Hadramauta v epohu drevnosti,* p. 220.
92 Bāfaqīh: *L'unification du Yémen antique*, p. 411.
93 Ibid.
94 Francuzov: *Istorija Hadramauta v epohu drevnosti,* p. 247.
95 Robin: "Quelques épisodes marquants," p. 63.

Thus, by the 4th century CE Ḥimyar became the dominant kingdom in South Arabia, taking control over the South Arabian territories and unifying by conquest the whole of south Arabia for the first time in history[96]. The aggressive policy of the Ḥimyarite kingdom was not limited to South Arabia however. Ḥimyar was the first South Arabian kingdom which managed to spread its influence beyond the region into central and western Arabia, with the exception of southern Ḥiğāz[97]. The Ḥimyarites also appointed a Kindite clan of Ḥuğr to serve as their proxy rulers over central Arabia[98].

Relations with nomadic northern tribes proved to be an important political factor[99]. Like other South Arabian kingdoms, Ḥimyar was forced to deal with nomadic raids, and tried to extend their control over them and to integrate into the social structure or to use them for military raids[100]. In order to achieve these goals, the Ḥimyarite kings conducted campaigns to the north. In the second half of the 5th century CE, this practice weakened and their campaigns came to a temporary halt[101].

In the 6th century, due to the protracted political crisis and increasing political fragmentation, the kingdom lost its political independence and was first acquired by Ethiopia and then by the Sassanid empires[102]. These events will be further analyzed in the subchapter „The political situation in the 6th century CE".

According to Korotayev, a distinctive feature of the Ḥimyarite Kingdom was a centralized state organization, which largely ensured its military successes[103]. Having unified South Arabia under their rule, the Ḥimyarites tried to implement their system of public administration.[104]. These attempts at centralization probably only increased resistance and caused uprisings, both of tribes and of noble families.

---

96 Hoyland: *Arabia and the Arabs*, p. 47.

97 Christian Robin: "Arabia and Ethiopia," *The Oxford Handbook of late Antiquity*. Ed. Scott Fitzgerald Johnson. New York: Oxford University Press, 2012, pp. 272-273.

98 Hoyland: *Arabia and the Arabs*, p. 49.

99 Robin: "La pénétration des Arabes nomades au Yémen," p. 72.

100 Hoyland: *Arabia and the Arabs*, p. 49.

101 Piotrovsky: *Juzhnaja Aravija v rannee srednevekov'e*, p. 20.

102 Hoyland: *Arabia and the Arabs*, p. 51.

103 Korotayev: *Social'naja istorija Jemena*, p. 52.

104 Ibid.

Having conquered South Arabia, the Ḥimyarites began to unify the region culturally and religiously as well, by imposing the Sabaic language and eventually by religious policy[105]. In the period after the conquest of other kingdoms, religious policy became an important instrument of political unification for Ḥimyar[106]. In the pantheons of ancient South Arabian kingdoms, the main deity played a significant role with which the members of the community identified themselves (for example, in familial terms)[107]. From this point of view, the gradual departure from polytheism, the reduction of the number of gods to one, can be considered in the context of religious policy. The kingdom of Ḥimyar in conditions of considerable diversity, according to Gajda, may have used monotheism as a tool that consolidated the social and tribal structure of the South Arabian society[108]. Similarly, the practice of establishing state religion should be taken into account when the king Yūsuf Asʾar Yaṯʾar introduced Judaism as the official religion in the Ḥimyarite kingdom[109].

Regarding their language policy, the Ḥimyarites adopted the Sabaic language for official purposes and it was used in Ḥimyarite inscriptions[110]. The opinions of scholars differ on the question of when exactly Sabaic became the language of the Ḥimyarite kingdom (Beeston argues that Sabaic was used in Ḥimyarite inscriptions from the 4th to the 6th century CE[111], while Kogan and Korotayev claim that the kingdom of Ḥimyar adopted Sabaic as official language in the late 1st century CE[112]). In any case, the idea of continuity with the Sabaean kingdom was clearly important for Ḥimyar.

As in the case of other kingdoms, the economy of the kingdom relied on agriculture with an irrigation system, as well as trade and exports of frankincense and myrrh[113]. The

105 Robin: "Arabia and Ethiopia," p. 270.
106 Gajda: *Le royaume de Himyar à l'époque monothéiste,* p. 12.
107 Christian Robin: "Du paganisme au monothéisme," *Revue du monde musulman et de la Méditerranée,* 61 (1991), p. 140.
108 Gajda: *Le royaume de Himyar à l'époque monothéiste,* p. 35.
109 Robin: "Arabia and Ethiopia,"p. 270.
110 Robin: " Les langues de la Péninsule Arabique," p. 95.
111 A.F.L. Beeston: "Languages of pre-Islamic Arabia," *Arabica,* Vol. 28, Issue 2 (1981), p. 179.
112 Kogan and Korotayev: "Sayhadic Languages, " p. 221.
113 Piotrovsky: *Juzhnaja Aravija v rannee srednevekov'e,* p. 37.

trading network of the kingdom of Ḥimyar was associated with the Mediterranean world and the East African coast[114].

1.1.6. Kinda

Kinda appeared north of Yemen in the 1st and 2nd century BCE and due to aggressive policies and raids became an obstacle and a threat to trade routes[115]. In order to protect trade routs, the Sabaean Kingdom and Ethiopia started a military campaign against Kinda[116]. Kinda actively subjugated tribes during the 2nd and 3rd century BCE. As a political structure, Kinda became tribal confederation, including nomadic and semi-nomadic tribes of Qaḥṭān and Maḏḥiǧ as well as the settled population of oases [117]. In the 3rd century CE Kinda made an unsuccessful raid on the Sabaean kingdom [118]. The tribe of Kinda is mentioned in historical sources in the third and early fourth century CE, when they formed an auxiliary military force for first the Sabaeans and then the Ḥimyarites[119].

In the 5th century CE, with the help of the Ḥimyarites, the Kinda formed a kingdom in central Arabia which was politically dependent on the Ḥimyarite kingdom[120]. In their expansionist policies, they reached the territories of the Laḫmids, but they were defeated by the Laḫmids in 529 CE. Internal political conflicts also played a role. As a result, a group of Kindites moved to Ḥaḍramawt, establishing political control over most of the territory, which provoked resistance and conflicts with other tribes[121].

---

114 Ibid., p.48.

115 Mikhail Bukharin: "Towards the earliest history of Kinda." *Arabian Archaeology and Epigraphy*, 20 (2009), p. 64.

116 Ibid., p. 65.

117 Al-Zahrani: *L'histoire des tribus Kinda et Madhhij*, p.11.

118 Christian Robin: "Le royaume hujride, dit « royaume de Kinda », entre Himyar et Byzance." *Comptes rendus des séances de l'Académie des Inscriptions et Belles-Lettres*, Vol. 140, N. 2 (1996), p. 666.

119 Christian Robin: "Les rois de Kinda," *Arabia, Greece and Byzantium. Cultural Contacts in Ancient and Medieval Times*. Eds. by Abdulaziz Al-Helabi [et al.]. Riyadh: King Saud University, Department of History, 2012, p. 62.

120 Al-Zahrani: *L'histoire des tribus Kinda et Madhhij*, p. 45.

121 Piotrovsky: *Juzhnaja Aravija v rannee srednevekov'e*, p. 61.

Even after the collapse of the kingdom, the leaders of the Kindites continue to play a significant role in Arabia. Majority of the Kindite army[122] also supported the Ethiopian ruler of Ḥimyar, ʾAbraha, when he launched an expedition against tribes in central and western Arabian in the mid-6th century CE[123].

1.2. THE POLITICAL SITUATION IN THE 6TH CENTURY CE

The political situation in the 6th century was determined by the growing level of political decentralization, the weakening of royal power and resistance by the nobility and tribes, as well as the growth of foreign political pressure. South Arabia was important as a section of the maritime trade route from the Mediterranean sea to India, which led to interest in it from neighboring countries.

Fragmentation and decentralization led to the weakening of the state power of the kingdom, while control mostly went to the tribal leaders. In turn, this intensified the tribal struggle and conflicts[124].

Thus, as mentioned earlier, the Ḥimyarite kingdom suffered a reversal of fortunes in the 6th century CE. Given the unstable internal political situation, the Ḥimyarite kingdom originally tried to preserve its independence and political neutrality. However, as the political crisis and fragmentation intensified, the rulers begin to seek foreign policy support due to the unstable political environment [125].

The adoption of Judaism as the state religion by Yūsuf Asʾar Yaṯʾar may be interpreted in this way. This step meant a political break with Ethiopia. The policy of Yūsuf Asʾar Yaṯʾar, including the religious policy, led to an immediate armed conflict. The

122 A notable exception was Yazid bin Kabšat, who rebelled against Abraha in the Ḥaḍramawt
123 Robin: "Le royaume hujride, dit « royaume de Kinda », entre Himyar et Byzance, " p.666
124 Al-Medej: *Yemeni relations*, pp. 17-18.
125 Piotrovsky: *Juzhnaja Aravija v rannee srednevekov'e*, p. 157.

resistance of the nobility, as well as the killing of Christians in Naǧrān played its role[126]. As a result, Yūsuf As'ar Yaṯ'ar lost and kingdom of Ḥimyar was conquered by Ethiopia and lost its political independence[127].

The conquest in the first place meant a turn in religious policy. The conquest led to the rejection of Judaism, as well as the persecution of the Jews[128]. During this period, parts of the aristocracy of the Jewish confession probably turned to Christianity, and Christianity became the official religion. On the other hand, the political system itself remained practically unchanged[129]. The name of the king who was placed by Aksum on the Ḥimyarite throne was Ma'dikarib Ya'fur, who reigned from 519 until 522 CE[130].

In general, during the period of the Ethiopian conquest, qayls and tribal chiefs often organized resistance or anti-Ethiopian movements, which however did not have serious consequences[131].

When 'Abraha became the king, he continued to use the Ḥimyarite title and to use the Sabaic language in inscriptions[132]. Thus, even during the Ethiopian conquest, continuity with the Ḥimyarite kingdom persisted in political, and mainly in cultural terms (with the exception of religious issues)[133]. In this case, 'Abraha, while formally recognizing the sovereignty of the Ethiopian king, conducted an autonomous policy [134].

Significant changes affected the sphere of foreign policy. The main focus of foreign policy was to mount military campaigns to the north and attack nomadic tribes.'Abraha later led the ill-fated assault on Mecca which ended in failure for Ḥimyar and probably propelled the tribe of Qurayš to the dominant position in western Arabia[135]. Despite the mutiny by the qayls in 541-542 CE, Abraha's rule as a whole was successful, but it only delayed the crisis.

126 Robin: "Nagrān vers l'époque du massacre, " p. 42.
127 Robin: "Arabia and Ethiopia,"p. 284.
128 Gajda: *Le royaume de Himyar à l'époque monothéiste,* p. 116.
129 Robin: "Arabia and Ethiopia,"p. 283.
130 Ibid., p. 281.
131 Al-Medej: *Yemeni relations*, p. 5.
132 Piotrovsky: *Juzhnaja Aravija v rannee srednevekov'e,* p. 23.
133 Gajda: *Le royaume de Himyar à l'époque monothéiste,* p. 116-146.
134 Nebes: "Die Märtyrer von Nagrān," p. 29.
135 Robin: "Arabia and Ethiopia," p. 286.

After his death, the qayls tried to resist the Ethiopian domination and sought foreign support. Thus, the vassal kingdom of Ethiopia ceased to exist around 570-575[136]. As a result of this struggle, Ḥimyarites couldn't regain control over the entire territory, some of which was under the control of Sassanid Persians[137].

Despite attempts at resistance, including those led by the son of ʾAbraha[138], the Sassanid Persians conquered most of the territory of South Arabia. Formally, all of South Arabia became part of the Sassanid Empire, but parts of the territories were actually controlled by the tribal chiefs[139]. Sassanid Empire maintained control of the region until the rise of the Islamic state[140].

1.3. THE DECLINE OF SOUTH ARABIA

By the time of Islam appeared in the region, South Arabia witnessed not only a radical political and cultural change, but an overall decline in population density as well[141].All the major South Arabian cities either suffered a serious decline or were depopulated altogether: Šabwa, the former capital of Ḥaḍramawt, was almost entirely abandoned in the 5th century; Sabaean capital of Mārib lost its original influence after the Ḥimyarite conquest and was abandoned following the collapse of the Ḥimyarite state; Qaryat al-Fāw, the Kindite capital, was abandoned by the beginning of the 4th century[142]. Ḥimyarite capital of Ẓafār suffered a similar fate, experiencing population decline in the 6th century[143].

---

136 Ibid., p. 288.
137 Al-Medej: *Yemeni relations*, p. 6.
138 Piotrovsky: *Juzhnaja Aravija v rannee srednevekov'e*, p. 124.
139 Al-Medej: *Yemeni relations*, p. 6.
140 Robin: "Arabia and Ethiopia," p. 297.
141 Jérémie Schiettecatte: "L'évolution du peuplement sudarabique du Ier au VIe siècle." *L'Arabie à la veille de l'islam. Un bilan clinique*. Éd. Christian Robin et Jérémie Schiettecatte. Paris: Diffusion De Boccard, 2008 (Orient et Méditerranée, 3), p. 219.
142 Schiettecatte: "À la veille de l"islam," p. 11.
143 Ibid., 12.

According to Schiettecatte, the reasons for this population decline are multiple: desertification of the entire region, a long-lasting economic crisis, which started in the 3rd century CE and led to the abandonment of some port cities, as well as a tribal rejection of supra-tribal polities like Ḥimyar[144].

The climatic factor, specifically aridity, caused the deepening of the economic crisis in agriculture, which already had difficulties due to problems in the functioning of the irrigation systems[145]. It should be borne in mind that the construction and maintenance of such large-scale engineering structures were under state control. This made them vulnerable in the situation when the state apparatus was weakened by decentralization and mutual strife[146].

Another important branch of the economy, trade, also experienced a crisis. Due to the competition from other states, the loss of seaports, problems with the functioning of caravan routes, South Arabia ceased to play an important role in international trade routes[147]. On the other hand, this also affected the overall level of economic welfare.

The internal political factor that played a role in the decline is political fragmentation. Resistance of the nobility and conflicts of the tribes played their role in the political crisis of the Ḥimyarite state, and consequently in the establishment of foreign domination[148]. However, these factors created instability and were a threat to the established power of Ethiopia and Persia as well. Thus, political centralization continued to intensify, which led to a new round of conflicts and clashes between tribes[149].

Nomadic tribes played a role in the decline of South Arabia as well. Climatic and economic factors led to the advancement of the Bedouins to the south, which means that the state formations had to face a new wave of nomadic tribes. Weakness of the central state

144 Schiettecatte: "L'évolution du peuplement sudarabique du Ier au VIe siècle," pp. 217-249.
145 Piotrovsky: *Juzhnaja Aravija v rannee srednevekov'e,* p. 36.
146 Al-Medej: *Yemeni relations*, p. 18.
147 Jérémie Schiettecatte: "Ports et commerce maritime dans l'"Arabie du Sud préislamique." Chroniques yéménites, 15 (2008), p. 87.
148 Al-Medej: *Yemeni relations*, p. 17-18.
149 Schiettecatte: "L'évolution du peuplement sudarabique du Ier au VIe siècle," pp. 243-245.

apparatus made effective integration into social and political structures of the previous periods impossible. Thus, this new wave of nomadic tribes became another destabilizing factor[150].

The political history of the region is characterized by intense internal political struggle of various actors. On the one hand, the kingdoms fought among themselves, seizing each others territory, depriving each other of political independence and losing their own independence. As a result, the Ḥimyarite kingdom managed to unite the entire territory of South Arabia under its authority. On the other hand, conflicts occurred between tribes and tribal unions, as well as between sedentary and nomadic tribes. The raids of nomadic tribes played a role not only in the decline of the kingdoms, but also in the genesis of the tribal structure and social organization of South Arabian polities. After the Ḥimyarite conquest and the subordination of all South Arabian territories, they pursued a policy of unification, trying to transform the administrative structure of the subordinate territories. During this period, the resistance of aristocratic families and the struggle for power at the top of society were an important destabilizing factor. Together with economic difficulties, these internal political conflicts led to the fact that the kingdom of Ḥimyar was conquered and lost its political independence.

2. ECONOMY AND SOCIAL ORGANIZATION

The socio-economic development of the region, like the political development, is characterized by alternating periods of prosperity and crisis. This subchapter addresses the main branches of the economy, as well as a brief history of the region's economic development. The second part of the subchapter is devoted to social organization. The distinctiveness of the social organization of South Arabian society lies in its complex character, which provided for several vertical structures associated with different spheres of life. This section analyzes the social structures of tribes and states, as well as various interpretations of key terms related to it.

---

150 Piotrovsky: *Juzhnaja Aravija v rannee srednevekov'e*, p. 52.

2.1. ECONOMIC DEVELOPMENT

In general, the economy of South Arabia during this period was characterized by highly developed agriculture and cattle breeding with extensive use of artificial irrigation techniques[151]. Also construction, stone carving, manufacture of handicrafts (weapons, leather goods, fabrics, clothes) were developed in the region and were highly valued outside the region[152].

Handicraft production and demand for it from outside the region were among the factors that determined the particular importance of trade. The importance of trade routes was a political factor, with the result that the state and the tribe tried to monopolize the trade routes. With the consolidation and centralization of power, economic control over the roads and ports was established as well[153].

The development of trade was conditioned by internal factors as well. South Arabia itself included several geographical zones, which necessitated a trade exchange between them. Intra-trade ties were particularly dependent on political processes: they were strengthened during periods of political centralization and weakened during periods of fragmentation[154].

South Arabia was also the center of transit trade. Control over trade transit through Arabia, as well as trade in incense was of international importance. Ancient South Arabia was the main source of frankincense and myrrh, which were traded by an overland trade route to the rest of the Mediterranean world[155]. This overland trade can be divided into two phases; the first lasted from the 6th to the 2nd century BCE, which was mostly under the control of the Minaean kingdom and is very well attested by South Arabian inscriptions, and the second one

151 Ibid., p.36

152 Ibid., p.46.

153 Beeston: "The Arabian Aromatics Trade in Antiquity," p. 57.

154 Piotrovsky: *Juzhnaja Aravija v rannee srednevekov'e,* p. 47.

155 Beeston: "The Arabian Aromatics Trade in Antiquity," p. 53.

which lasted from the 1st century BCE to the 1st century CE[156], when the overland route was mostly supplanted by maritime trade[157].

Trade in incense was a source of prosperity. However, competition from Egypt due to the development of maritime trade, and later from the Roman Empire, weakened the importance of the overland trade routes in South Arabia. This affected the decline of cities along the caravan routes, which, moreover, could no longer effectively resist the onslaught of nomadic tribes [158].

At the same time, this competition influenced the development of sea trade as well. While cities along the caravan routes began to decline, the ports began to expand and flourish. In the 1st and 2nd century CE sea trade is flourishing[159].

However, the weakening of transit trade with India due to competition with Egypt stimulated the export of Yemeni products. On the other hand, the drop in demand for Yemeni goods in the Mediterranean led to an increase in its role in intra-Arabian trade[160].

The sea trade experienced a crisis in the 3rd century CE due to political instability deepened by the economic crisis in the entire Red Sea region, and only moderate development despite the positive dynamics in the 4-6th centuries CE[161].

Because of the political crisis and military conquests, South Arabian trade finally ceased to play a role in international trade networks. Under the changing circumstances, South Arabia could not compete effectively with other regions and states, and in the end the state was unable to provide for the functioning of the caravan routes and lost its control of the coast and ports.

The economic crisis affected also another important economic sector, namely agriculture. On the one hand, political fragmentation and crises led to the state being unable to

---

156 Ibid.
157 Schiettecatte: "À la veille de l"islam," p. 10.
158 Schiettecatte: "L'évolution du peuplement sudarabique du Ier au VIe siècle," p. 242.
159 Schiettecatte: "Ports et commerce maritime dans l"Arabie du Sud préislamique," p. 71.
160 Piotrovsky: *Juzhnaja Aravija v rannee srednevekov'e,* p. 48.
161 Schiettecatte: "Ports et commerce maritime dans l"Arabie du Sud préislamique," p. 84.

maintain the functionality of irrigation systems. As large-scale projects, irrigation systems were created on the initiative and under the control of the state authorities[162]. On the other hand, the environmental crisis and climatic factor also had an impact on the economic downturn in agriculture. Thus the economic crisis covered all sectors of the economy and became one of the factors in the decline of the region.

2.2. SOUTH ARABIAN COINAGE

The question of ancient South Arabian coinage is discussed in detail in the articles of the collection *Coinage of the Caravan Kingdoms*, edited by Huth and van Alfen[163]. The beginning of coinage in South Arabia is connected with the kingdoms Saba᾽ and Qatabān, in both cases their coinage was an imitation of Athenian coins [164]. Most of these South Arabian imitations were minted under the circumstances of the intensive overland caravan trade (4th to the 2nd century BCE)[165]. According to Peter van Alfen and his detailed die study of these coinages, despite their conceptual similarities and mutual influence, it is impossible that the coins were minted by the same political authorities[166].

Later coins were produced in the period when the aromatics trade began to shift from overland to maritime trade and the minting of coinage slowed down (late 2nd and early 1st century BCE)[167]. No local South Arabian coins were produced in the period of Ḥimyarite domination over the region between the 3rd and 6th century CE, and instead only foreign,

162 Piotrovsky: *Juzhnaja Aravija v rannee srednevekov'e*, p. 169.
163 Martin Huth and Peter G. van Alfen: "Introduction." *Coinage of the Caravan Kingdoms: Studies in the Monetization of Ancient Arabia*. Eds. M. Huth and P. van Alfen. New York: American Numismatic Society, 2010 (Numismatic Studies 25), pp. 1-25.
164 Martin Huth: "Athenian Imitations from Arabia." *Coinage of the Caravan Kingdoms: Studies in the Monetization of Ancient Arabia*. Eds. M. Huth. P. van Alfen. New York: American Numismatic Society, 2010 (Numismatic Studies 25), pp. 227-256.
165 Huth and van Alfen: "Introduction," p.7.
166 van Alfen, Peter: "Die Studies of the Earliest Qatabanian and Sabaean Coinages." *Coinage of the Caravan Kingdoms: Studies in the Monetization of Ancient Arabia*. Eds. M. Huth and P. van Alfen. New York: American Numismatic Society, 2010 (Numismatic Studies 25), p. 272.
167 Schiettecatte: "Ports et commerce maritime dans l"Arabie du Sud préislamique," p. 83.

Byzantine and Aksumite coins were used[168], however in the earlier period some Sabaeo-Ḥimyarite 'Royal' series were minted, which bore the names of rulers which issued them[169]. The previously mentioned period of crisis in economic development affected the demonetization of the economy as well[170].

2.3. SOCIAL ORGANIZATION

South Arabian society is characterized by a complex social organization, which included several vertical structures associated with different spheres of life. The social structure was determined by the distribution of power and the specifics of state organization on the one hand, and the organization of tribal communities, tribes and their unions on the other[171]. Particular elements of the social structure were the nomadic tribes and the urban population[172].

From the point of view of the distribution of power, the system of social stratification included the following elements: the king, nobles (*qayls*, governors, officials), dependent state subjects (dependent on the king, *qayl* or *ša'b* community), while providing for several degrees of servitude[173].

However, the distinctiveness of this stratification was determined by the social structure of communities, which are the basic element of social organization.

168 Huth and van Alfen: "Introduction," p.9.

169 Christian Robin, "Himyarite kings on coinage." *Coinage of the Caravan Kingdoms: Studies in the Monetization of Ancient Arabia*. Eds. M. Huth. P. van Alfen. New York: American Numismatic Society, 2010 (Numismatic Studies 25), pp.357-383.

170 Schiettecatte: "À la veille de l''islam," p. 10.

171 Piotrovsky: *Juzhnaja Aravija v rannee srednevekov'e*, p. 71.

172 Lundin: *Juzhnaja Aravija v VI veke*, p. 94.

173 Robin: "Before Himyar," p. 95.

Pre-Islamic South Arabia was based around the community known as *byt*, which could mean a kind of territorial community or its place of living[174]. Two key questions about the nature of this form of social organization:

- The nature of the settlement. Beeston claims that *byt* is a village community. On the other hand, Korotayev indicates that such type of Sabaic settlement as *hgr* (which can be considered as more urban type) were also consisted of *byt*s[175]

- Whether *byt* is a kinship group [176]. *Byt* had a predominantly territorial character, it is likely that kinship and genealogical links did not play a significant role.

Korotayev singles out the following components in his analysis of stratification within *byt*: the clan nucleus (with leading group patriarch and his relatives), the female part (the wives of the members of the "clan nucleus"), the "unfree" members, the clients and personal assistants of the clan leaders[177].

Multiple *byts* were united into a *š'b*. The first problem of this term is the wide range of meanings: from tribe to province[178]. According to Robin, the exact meaning of the term can depend on the context in which the term was used or on the territory to which the term is applied[179].

Korotayev proposes to divide this term in three levels (order). In the narrowest sense – local community. He describes them as «quite compact autonomous territorial entities with a marked central settlement (*hgr*)»[180]. Grouping of several such local communities into a unit

---

174 Beeston: "Kingship in Ancient South Arabia," p. 257.

175 Korotayev: *Social'naja istorija Jemena,* p. 21.

176 Beeston: "Kingship in Ancient South Arabia," p. 257.

177 Andrey Korotayev: "Internal Structure of Middle Sabaean Bayt." *Arabian Archaeology and Epigraphy*, 5 (1994), pp. 174–183.

178 Korotayev: *Social'naja istorija Jemena,* p. 16.

179 Robin: "Esquisse d'une histoire de l'organisation tribale en Arabie du Sudantique," p. 21.

180 Korotayev: *Pre-Islamic Yemen*, p. 18.

forms *š'b* as "tribe" (Korotayev uses Malinowski's term 'tribe-state' for them and emphasizes its political component)[181]. The next version of the term Korotaev connects with another term of Malinowski, the "tribe-nation" and describes it as a cultural community [182]. For them, Robin uses terms „confédération"[183]. Beeston considers unification on a socio-political basis as the next element of the social structure (mainly as a result of the establishment of control by one tribe over neighboring ones) and calls this form commonwealth[184].

An important term for the analysis of social structure is *qayl.* Initially, the head of the *š'b* was designated by the title of *kabir*, but they were gradually forced out of power by the *qayls*[185]. Piotrovsky refers to the transition period, when one person was both the generic head of the *ša'b* and the royal governor i.e. *qayl*[186]. Sometimes they were descendants from the ancient tribal aristocracy or servicemen (government official). Among their functions in the *ša'b* is the military command of the militia as well as organization of general works, such as maintenance of the irrigation system[187].

Piotrovsky argues that it is difficult to analyze the social structure of ancient South Arabian society and, as an example, demonstrates that a part of the *ša'b* was directly dependent on the *qayl*[188]. According to Korotaev, such communities had the same devices as *bayt*[189]. They acted like a tribal administrative center. According to Korotaev such administrative functions were performed by their *mqtwy* ("personal assistants") and clients. That is, they acted as "proto-officials»[190].

As for their relationship with the royal authorities, opinions differ. Korotayev points out that "the *qayls* were not the agents of royal power"[191]. According to Piotrovsky, the *qayls* were subordinate to the kings, appointed by them, and carried out their assignments, but as the

---

181 Korotayev: *Social'naja istorija Jemena,* p. 17.

182 Korotayev, A. V., «The Political Role of the Sha'b of the First Order», Raydan. 6 (1994): 47–52.

183 Robin: "Esquisse d'une histoire de l'organisation tribale en Arabie du Sudantique," p. 22.

184 A. F. L.Beeston: "Some Features of Social Structure in Saba. *Studies in the History of Arabia. Vol. I. Sources for the History of Arabia.* Ed. A.M. Abdallah, et al. Riyadh: University of Riyadh, 1979, p. 117.

185 Piotrovsky: *Juzhnaja Aravija v rannee srednevekov'e,* p. 74.

186 Ibid., 141.

187 Korotayev: *Social'naja istorija Jemena,* p. 29.

188 Piotrovsky: *Juzhnaja Aravija v rannee srednevekov'e,* p. 141.

189 Korotayev: *Social'naja istorija Jemena,* p. 30.

190 Ibid.

191 Ibid., p. 35.

fragmentation and deepening political crisis grew, the *qayls* often opposed royal power, they could organize an uprising or try to become kings themselves[192].

Separately, the presence of urban self-government should be noted. The social organization of urban settlements included an appointed royal governor, free city dwellers (of whom city chiefs were appointed and elected), city day laborers, rural tenants and slaves.

3. CULTURE AND RELIGION

This section is devoted to the cultural heterogeneity of the ancient South Arabia. The section deals with the specificity of various languages, their prevalence and the problem of the linguistic domination. The role of languages and their use in the cultural policy of South Arabian states is analyzed as well. The second part of the section is devoted to questions of religion. First of all, the characteristics of ancient South Arabian polytheism are considered, including such issues as the structure of the pantheon, the functions of deities and the role of the pantheons themselves in terms of political self-identification. Secondly, the transition to monotheism, including from the point of view of its political significance, will be analyzed. The last part of this section is devoted to Judaism and Christianity. It includes consideration of such issues as the prevalence of these religions in the region, their influence on the formation of monotheism, as well as their role in political history of South Arabia.

3.1. ANCIENT SOUTH ARABIAN LANGUAGES

The four languages in which the pre-Islamic South Arabian inscriptions were written were Sabaic, Qatabānic, Hadramitic and Minaic, which besides similarities between them could be distinguish on the basis of morphological differences[193]. The earliest inscriptions

---

192 Piotrovsky: *Juzhnaja Aravija v rannee srednevekov'e*, p. 74.

193 Robin: " Les langues de la Péninsule Arabique," p. 93.

appeared ca. 1000-900 BCE[194], a significant number of confirmed documents can be attributed to the 8th century BCE (Sabaic and Minaic)[195]. At the same time, since the end of the 4th century CE, there has been a significant foreign influence and borrowings from the Greek and Aramaic[196]. The latest documents date from the second half of the 6th century. Writing culture ceased to exist after the Ethiopian conquest[197]. Of all languages, Sabaic is most similar to Arabic, Minaic and Qatabānic differ to some extent, and Hadramitic differs radically from it.[198]

3.1.1. Sabaic

Of these four languages, Sabaic seems to be the closest to Arabic[199]. It was originaly distributed in the region of Ma'rib and Ṣirwâḥ, it was the main language of the Sabaean kingdom, and it managed to survive the fall of the kingdom of Saba[200]. The phenomenon of "pseudo-Sabaean language" appeared among the neighboring Arabian tribes (in Najrān, Ḥaram and Qaryat al-Fāw) in the second century BCE. According to Robin, this language wasn't connected with the political influence of the kingdom of Saba, but with its religious practices [201].

Since Sabaic was also widely used as a language of other south Arabian inscriptions due to its cultural prestige and significant traditions , it survived as such medium until the 6th century CE[202]. In the same way Sabaic was adopted by Ḥimyar and was used in Ḥimyarite inscriptions[203]. According to Beeston, Sabaic was used in Ḥimyarite inscriptions from the 4th

---

194 P. Stein : " Palaeography of the Ancient South Arabian script. New evidence for an absolute chronology," *Arabian Archaeol Epigraphy*, 24 (2013), pp. 186–195.

195 Kogan and Korotayev: "Sayhadic Languages, " p. 220.

196 Ibid.

197 Ibid., p. 221.

198 Robin: "Arabia and Ethiopia,"p. 251.

199 Robin: " Les langues de la Péninsule Arabique," p. 95.

200 Ibid., 96.

201 Ibid., 97.

202 Beeston: "Languages of pre-Islamic Arabia," p. 179

203 Robin: " Les langues de la Péninsule Arabique," p. 95.

century CE and in the previous period the Ḥimyarite area did not fall into the sphere of "Sabaic literate culture"[204]. Presumably, Qatabānic language was used in Ḥimyarite inscriptions in the first period or, on the other hand, it can be considered as modified variant of Sabaic[205]. Kogan and Korotayev claims that the kingdom of Ḥimyar adopted Sabaic as official language in the late 1st century CE[206]. The idea of continuity with the Sabaean kingdom was important for Ḥimyar. Thus the Sabaic language finally displaced the Qatabānian in the territory of South Arabia by the 4th century CE, becoming the dominant language of the region.

However, it is debatable whether the language of the inscriptions was the language of everyday communication. Peter Stein argues that Late Sabaic was still connected with everyday form of communication[207]. On the other hand, the language of the inscriptions did not reflect conversational practice[208]. The prevalence and influence of the Sabaic language affected it's linguistic evolution, and as a result of this phenomenon a special form of Sabaic language arose, which was suitable for intertribal communication[209]. Due to this fact, Sabaic was also used by the tribes Qaḥtān, Maḏḥiğ, possibly Kinda as welll[210]. At the same time, because of the temporal and spatial spread of the language, the researchers have identified different phases of its development (Early-Middle-Late) and different dialects (North Central South).[211]

3.1.2. Minaic (Madhābic)

---

204 Beeston: "Languages of pre-Islamic Arabia," p. 179

205 Peter Stein: "The 'Ḥimyaritic' Language in preislamic Yemen – A Critical Re-evaluation." *Semitica et Classica*, 1 (2008), p. 203.

206 Kogan and Korotayev: "Sayhadic Languages, " p. 220.

207 P. Stein, "The 'Ḥimyaritic' Language in preislamic Yemen, " p. 205.

208 Christian Robin: "Les inscriptions de l'arabie antique et les études arabes." *Arabica,48* / 4 (2001), p. 510.

209 Beeston: "Languages of pre-Islamic Arabia," p. 180.

210 Robin: " Les langues de la Péninsule Arabique," p. 97.

211 Peter Stein: "Zur Dialektgeographie des Sabäischen." *Journal of Semitic Studies,* 49/2 (2004), p. 228.

Minaic was the language, which was used primarily in the Wādī Madhāb in the Yemeni Jawf. Predominantly it is known as the language of the kingdom of Maʿīn, however it was used by other communities in Wādī Madhāb as well[212]. The earliest Minaean inscriptions are attested around 8th century BCE[213]. For this reason, it is called Madhabic language. Robin claims that probably Mineans adopted for writing purposes language, which were already in use in the Wādī Madhāb[214]. His hypothesis is that the spoken language was different from the written[215].

Thanks to the trade links of the kingdom of Ma'īn, the distribution area is even wider. including the Minaean merchant colonies[216]. His disappearance occurred along with the fall of the kingdom of Maʿīn in 120 BCE when it disappeared[217]. A specific dialect of the Sabaean with a significant Arab influence was formed in his area[218], while the language itself differs significantly from both.

3.1.3. Qatabānian

Qatabānian was the language of the Qatabānian kingdom; its main distribution area were Wādī Bayhān and Wādī Ḥarīb on the edge of the inner Sayhad desert[219], although it was wider due to the political influence of the Qatabān kingdom. Accordingly, the majority of the inscriptions were created during the political domination of Qatabān. The language disappeared along with the disappearance of the kingdom of Qatabān, circa 175 CE[220].

---

212 Kogan and Korotayev: "Sayhadic Languages, " p. 220.
213 Ibid.
214 Robin: " Les langues de la Péninsule Arabique," p. 98.
215 Ibid.
216 Kogan and Korotayev: "Sayhadic Languages, " p. 220.
217 Robin: " Les langues de la Péninsule Arabique," p. 98.
218 Kogan and Korotayev: "Sayhadic Languages, " p. 221.
219 Ibid.
220 Robin: " Les langues de la Péninsule Arabique," p. 98.

3.1.4. Ḥaḍramitic

The language was distributed in Wādī Ḥaḍramawt and some adjoining areas. Ḥaḍramitic seems to have been the most divergent of all South Arabian languages, as well as the least studied with a small amount of attested inscriptions [221]. It was used approximately from 4th century BC to the period between 3rd and 4th century CE, and it disappeared along with the Ḥaḍramitic kingdom, around the beginning of the 4th century CE[222]

3.2 RELIGION IN SOUTH ARABIA

South Arabia had experienced a conversion to monotheism prior to the arrival of Islam. The polytheistic beliefs prevalent in South Arabia were diverse and reflected the complex social structure of the ancient society. This subchapter will briefly describe both the polytheistic religion as well as the evolution of religious views which led to the emergence of monotheism. The second part of the subchapter is devoted to the spread of Judaism and Christianity, including the specific features of religious policy and its consequences, as well as the political factors affecting, among others, the choice of religion on a state level.

3.2.1 Polytheism

Our knowledge of polytheistic religion of south Arabia is based primarily on the epigraphic evidence. The worship of various deities functioned on three levels: communal, state and general [223]. These levels were closely related: the deities of the communities acted as hypostasis and the regional characterization of the gods of other levels[224]. Different state formations and tribes had their pantheons of deities, consisting of different gods and

---

221 Ibid., 99.
222 Ibid., 98.
223 Piotrovsky: *Juzhnaja Aravija v rannee srednevekov'e,* p. 7.
224 Ibid.

goddesses[225]. The main deity of the pantheon was of key importance. According to Robin, this structure of the pantheon acted as an additional unifying factor, ensuring unity: for example, the patron deity of Qatabān was ʿAmm, whereas the patron of Saba' was the aforementioned ʾAlmaqah for Hadramawt - Sayyin (S'yn), for Maïn, - cAthtar dhu-Qabd (cttr d-Qbdm ou cttr d-Qbd). [226]. The main deity had its own temple, a center of religious life, which became the object of pilgrimage

Pagan beliefs were associated with planetary representations, so in most cases the main deity was connected with the moon or the sun[227]. Ordinary deities of the pantheon were of an animistic or ancestral nature[228]. Collective rituals were performed for the worship of ordinary deities. Many of them had their specific functions. However, on the whole, the question of the functions of various gods remains controversial. Unfortunately, the scarcity of information contained in the inscriptions doesn't give us even a rudimentary picture of the nature of these deities, since the only characteristics of the deities which the inscriptions provide us with are the familial relations (rare) either between the deities themselves, or between the deities and the tribes which worshiped them. Probably, the main god of the pantheon didn't have any specific functions, so believers could turn to him with different requests[229]. In addition to deities, religious beliefs included envoys between worlds and defenders of evil.

3.2.2. Conversion to monotheism

Monotheistic inscriptions started to appear during 4th century CE[230]. Pagan formulations cease to occur in the inscriptions, the number of references to deities is

---

225 Robin: "Du paganisme au monothéisme," p. 140.
226 Ibid.
227 Al-Medej: *Yemeni relations*, p.6.
228 Ibid,
229 Robin: "Du paganisme au monothéisme," p. 141.
230 A. Prioletta: " A new monotheistic inscription from the Military Museum of Ṣanʿā," in *New research in archaeology and epigraphy of South Arabia and its neighbors*. Proceedings of the "Rencontres Sabéennes 15" held in Moscow, May 25th –27th, 2011. Ed. by A.V. Sedov. Moscow: The State Museum of Oriental Art, 2012, pp. 315-332.

reduced, and the number of inscriptions in the temples is reduced as well. However, the religious rituals of the previous period are preserved in an altered form[231]. Polytheism is replaced by a monotheistic cult. According to Piotrovsky, this transformation is associated with the strengthening of the role of the main deity. At the first stage, a new one god is mentioned in old pagan formulations. Different inscriptions at the initial stage contain different variants of naming this one god. The inscriptions written after the late 4th century CE contain a number of religious terms of Hebrew origin[232]. In general, contact with Jews and Christians influenced both the transformation of the cult itself and the naming of the deity. [233]

The problem of studying the evolution of religious beliefs is related to a lack of information. The inscriptions do not reflect the situation with religious practices of all strata of society. Thus, research is possible only from the position of the ruling class. From this point of view, the development of monotheism is associated with changes in religious views of aristocracy and rulers, which were, in turn, dictated not so much by religious as by political reasons.

According to Iwona Gajda, the acceptance of monotheism was used as a political instrument of unification[234]. Gajda examining the implications of the adoption of monotheism in the policies of the kingdom, Gajda demonstrates its consolidating effect on the social and tribal structure of the South Arabian society. As noted above, polytheistic religious concepts were diverse, since pantheons, deities and rituals differed even at the community level[235]. At the same time, the presence of the pantheon was an important factor in the cohesion and self-identification of a society. Thus, the transition to monotheism, the standardization of worship and appeals to God also had a consolidating effect, but already on a national level. On the

231 A.F.L. Beeston: "The Religions of Pre-Islamic Yemen." L'Arabie du Sud. Histoire et Civilisation, vol. I: Le peuple Yemenite et ses raciness. Ed. J. Chelhod. Paris, 1984 (Islam d'hier et d'aujourd'hui, 21), p. 267.

232 Robin: "Arabia and Ethiopia," p. 270.

233 Krzysztof Kościelniak: "Jewish and Christian religious influences on pre-Islamic Arabia on the example of the term RḤMNN ("the Merciful")." *Orientalia Christiana Cracoviensia*, 3 (2011), p. 68.

234 Gajda: *Le royaume de Himyar à l'époque monothéiste*, p. 12.

235 Robin: "Du paganisme au monothéisme," p. 140.

other hand, the transition to monotheism could also have economic advantages for the Ḥimyarite kingdom, since it allowed the state to seize the property of the temples [236].

On the one hand, the transition to monotheism could have been the result of internal tendencies and the evolution of religious ideas. The structure of the pantheon with the main deity performing various functions was transformed in favor of strengthening the role of the main deity and the gradual withering away of the others due to fact that the main deity adopted the functions of the lower deities. On the other hand, the development of monotheism could have occurred under the influence of other monotheistic religions, primarily Christianity and Judaism[237].

At the first stage, monotheism in South Arabia can be described as indeterminate[238]. Existing in a cultural field which was under the influence of Judaism and Christianity, South Arabian monotheism remained nebulous. This religious uncertainty can also be explained by political motives. The detachment of rulers from existing religious systems demonstrates their desire to remain aloof and not to be affiliated with the states with which these systems were connected[239].

At the second stage, this indefinite monotheism gives way to Judaism and Christianity[240]. From the political point of view, this turn can be explained by the deepening of the political crisis and political fragmentation. Under the conditions of an unstable political situation, different groups sought foreign policy contacts, declaring their political preferences, including with the help of religious affiliation[241].

3.2.3 Judaism

236 Robin: "Arabia and Ethiopia," p. 270.
237 Kościelniak: "Jewish and Christian religious influences," p. 69.
238 Piotrovsky: *Juzhnaja Aravija v rannee srednevekov'e,* p. 105.
239 Ibid., 106.
240 Robin: "Du paganisme au monothéisme," p. 142.
241 Piotrovsky: *Juzhnaja Aravija v rannee srednevekov'e,* p. 108.

Initially, Judaism appeared in South Arabia as a result of the relocation of several Jewish communities into the region around the 1st century CE. Judaism gradually began to spread in South Arabian society, including a part of the nobility (3rd to 4th centuries CE)[242]. Judaism influenced the formation of monotheistic ideas in South Arabia. During the transformation of polytheism into monotheism, Jewish religious terms influenced the inscriptions containing references to the one god [243].

The rejection of polytheism, despite the considerable Jewish influence at the initial stage, did not affect the official status of Judaism[244]. Despite the growth in the number of followers among the nobility, religious beliefs, although becoming monotheistic, retained their non-denominational monotheistic character on the state level. On the one hand, this is determined by the policy of maneuvering in the foreign policy aspect. On the other hand, this may also be due to an attempt to maintain the loyalty of the Christian population of the kingdom.

However, despite the uncertainty in the initial stage of the transition to monotheism, the religious policy of the Ḥimyarite kingdom gradually gravitated towards Judaism. Among the political factors behind this choice, political ambitions in strengthening the influence in other regions of Arabia, where the positions of Judaism were already strengthened, can be taken into account, as well as the already mentioned opposition to the Ethiopian influence.[245] At the same time, since it was mainly spreading among the nobility, Judaism did not form stable groups either in the tribal or in the regional sense [246].

The decisive strengthening of Judaism occurred at the beginning of the 6th century CE, when Yūsuf Asʾar Yaṯʾar introduced Judaism as the official religion in the Ḥimyarite kingdom[247]. Such an important step is also connected with the political circumstances. The adoption of Judaism as a state religion can be seen as a manifestation of the struggle against Ethiopian influence. In addition, the policy of Dhū Nuwās, including the religious policy, led

---

242 Ibid.

243 Robin: "Arabia and Ethiopia," p. 270.

244 Robin: "Arabia and Ethiopia," p. 264.

245 Robin, Christian: "Le judaïsme de Ḥimyar." *Arabia*, 1 (2003), pp. 97-172.

246 Al-Medej: *Yemeni relations*, p.8.

247 Robin: "Arabia and Ethiopia," p. 270.

to an immediate armed conflict. The political defeat of Ḏū Nuwās in this conflict led to the rejection of Judaism. During this period, the aristocracy of the Jewish confession turned to Christianity.

Particular attention of researchers is also attracted to the question of the role of Judaism in the religious practices of the Kinda tribe. Although Judaism had an official status and was more frequent among the Ḥimyarites[248]; it was for the Kindites that this adoption had significant political consequences, and also influenced the social organization of the tribe itself[249].

3.2.4. Christianity

Christianity penetrated the region in the 1st century in connection with trade activity by Christian merchants. Part of the nobility converted to Christianity in cities connected with trade routes[250].

According to Christian sources, the first official Christian mission arrived in Yemen during the reign of Byzantine Emperor Constantius II about 350 CE. According to them, as a result of this mission the Ḥimyarite king not only ordered the construction of three churches, but he himself adopted Christianity. However, this story is not attested in the South Arabian inscriptions.[251]

Christians dominated Naǧrān and the island of Suquṭra; they were also found in Maʾrib, in Ḥaḍramawt and, probably, in the coastal areas which face Ethiopia[252]. In Naǧrān, part of the population adopted Christianity as a result of their ties with the Persian empire, and they belonged to such Christological denominations as Nestorian Christianity[253]. Another

---

248 Lecker: "Judaism among Kinda and the Ridda of Kinda," p. 636.
249 Robin: "Les religions pratiquées par les membres de la tribu de Kinda (Arabie) à la veille de l'Islam," pp. 205.
250 Piotrovsky: *Juzhnaja Aravija v rannee srednevekov'e,* p. 107.
251 Robin: "Du paganisme au monothéisme," p. 147.
252 Ibid.
253 Robin: "Arabia and Ethiopia," p. 282.

part of the population converted to Christianity due to the missionary activity of monophysites, their numbers increased after the relocation of monophysites expelled from Byzantium[254].

Due to confessional differences, the Christian community cannot be regarded as a single actor, including in the foreign policy aspect. At that time, the trade elite were the conductors of Ethiopian influence, as most of the Christian clan nobility. The Nestorians were associated with Sasanid influence however, and accordingly the Sasanid conquest contributed to the short-lived strengthening of Nestorians.

The key episode not only in the history of the spread of the Christianity region, but also in the political history of this period as a whole, is the massacre of Christians in Nağrān committed by the Ḥimyarite king Ḏū Nuwās around BCE 523. This event is well documented and several studies have been dedicated to it. Norbert Nebes in the article "Die Märtyree von Nagrān und das Ende der Himyar. Zur politischen Geschichte Südarabiens im frühen sechsten Jahrhund » investigates the persecution in Nağrān. Nebes considers these events in the context of the political situation and religious policy of the Ḥimyarite Kingdom. He also analyzes the consequences of this event for the political crisis. For the history of the region, these events are important as an excuse for the invasion of the army of the Ethiopian kingdom[255]. The loss of political independence deepened the political crisis. From the point of view of religious policy, the Ethiopian conquest of South Arabia defined the dominant role of Christianity as the official religion in the region[256].

CHAPTER II. ANALYSIS OF HISTORICAL SOURCES

In this chapter, the evolution of the political, cultural and religious circumstances in ancient South Arabia will be more thoroughly discussed by a comparative analysis of the available historical sources.

254 Piotrovsky: *Juzhnaja Aravija v rannee srednevekov'e,* p. 108.
255 Robin: "Du paganisme au monothéisme," p. 147.
256 Ibid.

The chapter is divided into two parts, the first part analyzing the information about these tribes which can be found in the ancient South Arabian inscriptions, and the second part which will focus on the information about the same tribes which is found in the medieval Islamic historiography, primarily in the history of Abū Jaʿfar Muḥammad ibn Jarīr aṭ-Ṭabarī, *Tārīḫ al-Rusul wa-l-Mulūk*.

1. ANCIENT SOUTH ARABIAN INSCRIPTIONS

The main source of inscriptions used in this thesis is the Corpus of South Arabian inscriptions (CSAI), which is an online database of pre-Islamic South Arabian inscriptions. It contains approximately 7.500 texts in all four ancient South Arabian languages. The project is directed by Alessandra Avanzini and all texts have been digitized by her team at the University of Pisa.

The inscriptions in this database are divided chronologically into five phases, which roughly correspond to five different political periods of ancient South Arabian history: *phase A*, which spans from the early first millennium to the fourth century BCE i.e. the period of Sabaean domination; *phase B*, covering the period from the fourth to first century BCE, when Qatabān and Ḥaḍramawt contested Sabaean control of South Arabia; *phase C*, which covers the period from the first century BCE to the early second century CE; *phase D*, extends from the late second to the late century CE, when the kingdoms of Ḥimyar, Ḥaḍramawt and Sabaʾ fought for control of the region; and finally *phase E*, covering the last pre-Islamic period of South Arabia (fourth to sixth centuries CE), when the region was conquered and ruled by Ḥimyar.

The inscriptions which were written in Sabaic are further classified as: *Early Sabaic*, meaning they were written before the fourth century BCE; the inscriptions from the period between fourth – third century BCE to the fourth CE are classified as *Central Middle Sabaic*, if they are located in the territory of the kingdom of Saba, and *Southern Middle Sabaic*, if they are found in the high plateau south of the city of Ṣanʿāʾ; finally, the inscriptions dated to the last pre-Islamic period, between the fourth and sixth century CE, are classified as *Late Sabaic*.

1.1. al-Ašʿar (*ʾs²ʿrⁿ*)

The tribe of al-Ašʿar is mentioned in two inscriptions, DAI Barʾān 2000-1 (D) and Ja 635 (D). The first inscription, DAI Barʾān 2000-1, is written in Central Middle Sabaic language, it was written in the D period and it was discovered in Maʾrib. It's a dedicatory text in which S²ʿrm ʾwtr, king of Sabaʾ and son of ʿlhn Nhfn, expresses his gratitude to ʾlmqh for his victory against a number of tribes, among which al-Ašʿar is mentioned.

The second inscription, Ja 635, written in the same period and in the same language, is also a dedicatory text which is located in Maḥram Bilqīs. The inscription chronicles a victorious military campaign performed by S²ʿrm ʾwtr against numerous enemies, including a victory over al-Ašʿar in the region of Shrtᵐ.

Based on the small number of inscriptions which mention the name of this tribe, and the fact that both inscriptions which contain the name of al-Ašʿar place them on the list of the tribes defeated by Sabaʾ, it would seem that they didn't play an important role in pre-Islamic Arabia.

1.3. ʿAkk (*ʿkᵐ*)

The tribe of ʿAkk is mentioned in eight ASA inscriptions, seven of those dated to the D period and one final in the E period. The territory of this tribe was in the Tihama region in Yemen, and it bordered with the territory of the tribe of al-Ašʿar.[257]

---

[257] EI³, s.v. ʿAkk (W. Gaskell).

Ir 17 is a dedicatory inscription in which the authors of the inscription, S^{2}fʿṯ ʾs^{2}wʿ and his son Zydm ʾymn of the family Hmdn, ḏ-Fys^{2}n and S^{1}ʾrn, express gratitude to ʾlmqh for a successful military campaign in the service of S^{2}mr Yhrʿs^2, king of Sabaʾ and ḏu-Raydān, against a number of tribes, ʿAkk being among them.

Ir 19 is also a dedicatory text, written to express gratitude to ʾlmqh on behalf of ʾls^{2}rḥ Yḥḍb and his brother Yʾzl Byn, kings of Sabaʾ and ḏu-Raydān, who successfully waged war against ʿAkk, Ethiopians and ḏ-S^{1}hrtm.

Ir 69 is a chronicle of a successful war waged by ʾls^{2}rḥ Yḥḍb and his brother Yʾzl Byn, kings of Sabaʾ and ḏu-Raydān, against the Ethiopians, with Ḥimyar as the ally of the Sabaeans. The tribe of ʿAkk itself isn't mentioned in the text; however "the land of ʿkm" is mentioned as the location of a battle between the forces of Sabaʾ and Ḥimyar on one side and the armies of the Ethiopians and of ḏ-S^{1}hrtm on the other.

Ja 574 is a dedicatory inscription which further chronicles the wars waged by Sabaʾ and Ḥimyar against the Ethiopians. In this text, ʾls^{2}rḥ Yḥḍb and his brother Yzʾl Byn, kings of Sabaʾ and ḏu-Raydān, express gratitude for a successful military campaign against the Ethiopians and their allies from the tribe of ḏ-S^{1}hrtm. During this campaign, the Sabaeans defeated the military force comprising of the Aksumites, Gmdn, S^{1}hrtm as well as ʿAkk.

Ja 575 is another in the line of dedicatory texts which narrate the victorious war waged by Sabaʾ against the Ethiopians. In this inscription, ʾls^{2}rḥ Yḥḍb and his brother Yzʾl Byn, kings of Sabaʾ and ḏu-Raydān, defeated the forces of the Ethiopians and their allies ḏ-S^{1}hrtm and ʿAkk, killing or capturing their women and children. After this battle, the remnant of the Ethiopians and ʿAkk regrouped and assaulted the Sabaean army, but were soundly defeated and forced to flee.

Ja 649 narrates an assault ordered by S^{2}mr Yhrʿs^2, king of Sabaʾ and ḏu-Raydān, against the tribes of ʿAkk and ḏ-S^{1}hrtm, who were attacked in the fortress of ḏ-Rgzgzn, where they fought for a full day and night. The Sabaeans were victorious the next day, routing the forces of ʿAkk and ḏ-S^{1}hrtm and taking numerous captives, camels, sheep and cattle.

ʿAbadān 1 is a long inscription detailing the Ḥimyarite conquest of South Arabia, and it's dated to the year 470 of the Ḥimyarite era, which corresponds to 360 CE. The tribe of ʿAkk is mentioned briefly as the target of a successful military campaign waged by a king, presumably S²rḥbʾl. ʿAkk were assaulted and defeated in S²wryn and S³rdd, and forty three ʿAkk captives were taken.

The final inscription, CIH 325, which is dated to the year 559-560 CE according to the Ḥimyarite calendar, is, according to the cultural notes on the DASI web page, the last dated ASA inscription before the Persian conquest of South Arabia. It is a construction text which is fragmented and therefore difficult to completely decipher. The last line of the inscription contains mention of the border between two tribes, ʿAkk and Ḥgrm, presumably as the location of the construction works which are the topic of the text.

All of these texts paint a fairly clear picture of the role and allegiance of the tribe of ʿAkk in pre-Islamic South Arabia; they were an enemy of the Sabaean kingdom and an ally of the Ethiopian army, until they were finally conquered by Ḥimyar.

1.4. Ǧarm (*grm*)

The tribe of Ǧarm is mentioned in only one dedicatory inscription, Ja 660 (D), according to which the army of Ǧarm was dispersed from the town of Maʾrib by the Sabaean army, its soldiers captured and brought before the king of Sabaʾ. Like al-ʾAšʿar, the fact that this tribe is mentioned in only one inscription indicates that they played a minor role in ancient South Arabia.

1.5. Hamdān (*hmdn*)

Their territory of the tribe of Hamdān was north of Ṣan'ā', between Maʾrib and Nağrān to the east and the coast to the west.[258] The CSAI archive contains eleven ASA inscriptions which mention this tribe. Five older inscriptions (B 8934, CIH 305 (D) and Ja 2871 (C), written in Central Middle Sabaic, don't contain any information which might indicate the political role of the tribe in South Arabia or its relations with other tribes or polities of the era. B 8934 is a very small fragment of a text whose meaning and nature is indecipherable. CIH 305 is DASI's attempt at reconstruction based on an Arabic text found in al-Hamdānī's *al-Iklīl*; it is a construction text according to which ʿlhn Nhfn and ʾws³lt Rfs²n of the tribe of Hamdān restored and erected a building and its tower. Ja 2871 is also a construction text which mentions that Tbʿkrb, Ḥywm and their sons built the tower of Yfʿn with the help of the tribe of Hamdān. Ja 651 (D) is a dedicatory inscription which mentions a flood which destroyed two houses of the tribes Hamdān and Btʿ during the feast of ʾbhy in the town of Maʾrib. After this, S²mr Yhrʿs², king of Sabaʾ and ḏū-Raydān, ordered the Sabaean army to erect a dam to protect the city from the flood. RES 4176 is a legal decree in which Tʾlb Rym Yrḫm, Lord of Trʿt, proclaims a number of legal obligations. Among those, Tʾlb promised to provide with tithe, among which a single banquet in a year is to be provided by Ḥmdn.

MAFRAY-al-Miʿsāl 2 (D, 363 Ḥim, i.e. 253 CE) is the only inscription which mentiones the tribe of Hamdān which is written in Southern Middle Sabaic. It narrates the battle in the plain of Ḥurma, where Krbʾl ʾyfʿ, king of Sabaʾ and ḏu-Raydān, and his Ḥimyarite army fought and defeated the Sabaean army. The inscription states that, among the captives taken by the victorious Ḥimyarite army, was a steward of the Hamdān.

All of the following inscriptions were written in Late Sabaic and they are dated to the E period, according to the DASI system of dating. The first of them, Ir 71, is a short construction text which only mentions that a governor of Hamdān completed a number of residences. The author of the inscription appears to have been Jewish, because the text contains a monogram of the word "Shalom".

---

258 EI[3], s.v. Hamdān (J. Schleifer).

Ja 1028, Ry 507 and Ry 508, all dated to the year 633 according to the Ḥimyarite calendar, which corresponds to 523 CE, are commemorative texts which chronicle the wars conducted by the Jewish king Yws¹f ʾs¹ʾr Yṯʾr, known as Ḏu-Nuwas in Arabic sources, against the Ethiopians and other South Arabian Christians. Hamdān is mentioned in this inscription as one of the tribes which fought alongside Yws¹f ʾs¹ʾr Yṯʾr in the siege of Nagrān.

Ja 547+Ja 546+Ja 544+Ja 545 (E, 668 Ḥim), which corresponds to 558 CE is a construction text which commemorates the construction of the Maʾrib dam; the tribe of Hamdān was part of this project alongside a number of other tribes, under the authority of Abraha, king of Sabaʾ, ḏu-Raydān, Ḥaḍramawt and Ymnt.

Based on these inscriptions, it seems clear that the tribe of Hamdān was an ally or a vassal of Ḥimyar, and that at least some of the Hamdānids converted to Judaism before the coming of Islam.

1.6. Ḫawlan (*ḫwln*)

The tribe of Ḫawlān (*Ḫwln*) is the tribe which is attested in the largest number of ASA inscriptions out of all the tribes which are analyzed in this thesis. The name of Ḫawlān was used by three communities, namely the tribe which was located in Ṣirwāḥ and whose name was Ḫawlan Ḫāḍilum (*Ḫwln Ḫḍlm*), another tribe called Ḫawlān Gudādān (*Ḫwln Gddtn*) which was located in the region of Ṣaʿda, and a third tribe, which isn't attested as part of a compound name, whom Robin named „the southern Ḫawlān".[259]

M 247 is the only inscription mentioning Ḫawlan which is written in Minaic. It is also one of the few ASA inscriptions which mention more distant lands like Egypt and Assyria. It is both a construction text, commemorating the construction of a wall between two towers of

---

[259] Christian Robin: "Sabaʾ et la Khawlān du Nord (Khawlān Gudādān): l'organisation et la gestion des conquêtes par les royaumes d'Arabie méridionale." *Issledovanija po Aravii i islamu. Sbornik statej b čect' 70-letija Muhaila Borisoviča Piotrovskogo* [Studies on Arabia and Islam. A collection of papers in honour of Mikhail Borishovich Piotrovskij on the occasion of his 70th birthday]. Ed. Alexander V. Sedov. Moskva: Gosudarstvennyj Muzej Vostoka, 2014, pp. 156-158.

Ẓrbn and Lbʾn by two kabirs of Mṣrn, ʿmṣdq son of Ḥmʿṯt of Yfʿn and S¹ʿd son of ʿlg of Ḍfgn, and a dedicatory text which praises ʿṯtr ḏ-Qbḍm, Wdm and Nkrḥm for protecting the merchandise of the two kabirs during the wars between Saba' and Ḫawlan as well as Egypt and Persia.

The tribe of Ḫawlan is mentioned in four inscriptions written in Qatabānic, all of them are very short and none of them provide much information regarding the political history of this tribe.

BaBa al-Ḥadd 10 is very short and virtually unreadable, making its nature difficult to decipher; it aparenty mentions one qayl of Ḫawlan and his palmgrove. BaBa al-Ḥadd 2 (C) is a construction text which commemorates the construction of a water reservoir by Mḫṭrn ʾs¹ʾr, qayl of Radmān and Ḫawlan. BaBa al-Ḥadd 7 (C) again narrates how a qayl of Ḫawlan, acquired and planted a vineyards and a palmgrove in the valley Mʿrmm. Finally, YMN 7 is another construction text which mentions construction of water conducts in order to irrigate the valley of Rmḍw.

The largest number of inscriptions is written in Sabaic. In fifteen of these, the name Ḫawlan is attested as part of a compound name, either as Ḫawlān Ḫāḍilum or as Ḫawlān Gudādān, and the majority of them are dated to the D period.

ʿAbadān 1 is a very long chronicle of the Ḥimyarite campaigns against tribes mostly outside South Arabia, . Unfortunately, the inscription is unreadable in places; however, based on the context of the inscription, it seems that Ḫawlan ḏ-Ḥbb was on the side of the Himyarite army.

Fa 3 is a legal text which gives a rare glimpse into the process of incorporating individuals into a tribe; namely, the Sabaean king Ns²ʾkrb Yʾmn Yhrḥb allowed a number of individuals and their families to become members of the tribe of his vassals, the qayls of the tribe Ṣirwāḥ, Ḫawlan Ḫāḍilum and Hynn.

Ir 23, unlike most other ASA inscriptions, doesn't contain any mention of a military exploit or conquest. It is meant to express gratitude of its author, ʿmrm Yzd, qayl of the tribes of Ṣirwāḥ, Ḫawlān Ḫāḍilum and Hynn, steward of Ns^{2}ʾkrb Yʾmn Yhrḥb, king of Sabaʾ and ḏu-Raydān, to ʾlmqh for granting him male children.

Ir 28 is an account of a diplomatic mission conducted by S^{2}rḥʿṯt ʾs^{2}wʿ, qayl of the tribes Ṣrwḥ and Ḫawlān Ḫāḍilum, in service of Krbʾl Wtr Yhnʿm, king of Sabaʾ, ḏu-Raydān, Ḥaḍramawt and Ymnt. S^{2}rḥʿṯt ʾs^{2}wʿ was sent as a delegate to the Ethiopian king and safely returned accompanied by the Ethiopian delegation to the Ḥimyarite king.

Ja 635 mentions how Ḫawlān Ḫāḍilum assisted ʾbkrb ʾḥrs^{1}, a servant of S^{2}ʿrm ʾwtr, king of Sabaʾ and ḏu-Raydān, in one of his military expeditions. They took part in his successful attack on the tribe of Yḥbr, which took place on the border with the territory of ʾs^{1}d.

Ja 649 is authored by the qayl of the tribes Ṣrwḥ and Ḫawlān Ḫāḍilum. He conducted a number of successful military campaign in the service of S^{2}mr Yhrʿs^{2}, king of Sabaʾ and ḏu-Raydān. One target of his campaigns was the tribe of ʿkm who were, alongside the tribe ḏ-S^{1}hrtm, assaulted and made to surrender in the fortress ḏ-Rgzgzn.

CIAS 39.11/o 3 n° 8 is one of the rare ASA inscriptions which was authored by a woman who expresses her gratitude to ʾlmqh Ṯhwn for the safe return of her husband, Rbbns^{1}rm ʾwḥs^{2}, who served in the Sabaean army in the town of Ṣʿdtm and the land of Ḫawlān Gudādān.

FB-Maḥram Bilqīs 2 is dated to the first half of the 3rd century CE, during the reign of the Sabaean king Lḥyʿṯt Yrḫm, and it recounts a punitive expedition conducted by his vassal Wafī Adhraḥ ibn Kabsī, the qayl of Tanʿim and Tanʿimat, against the Ethiopian army. The Ethiopians had pillaged the vassals of Lḥyʿṯt Yrḫm in Sihām, and the expedition was mounted as a response to this attack. Members of Ḫawlān Gudādān were among those who took part in this expedition.

Ja 576+Ja 577 is a very long account of a war led by ʾls^{2}rḥ Yḥḍb and his brother Yʾzl Byn, the two kings of Sabaʾ and ḏu-Raydān, against their Ethiopian enemies and their allies. Unfortunately, the inscription is damaged and therefore certain passages cannot be read. The tribe of Ḫawlān Gudādān is mentioned in this text, but because the part of the inscription where this tribe is mentioned is damaged, it is impossible to determine the role which this tribe played in these events.

Ja 601 and Nāmī NAG 7 are two identical inscriptions which (is the earliest dated mention of the tribe) Ḫawlān Gudādān is the target of the expeditions ordered by Wtrm Yhʾmn, king of Sabaʾ and ḏu-Raydān, against them as reprisal for certain offences which aren't mentioned in any detail in the text. Ḫawlān Gudādān were defeated and routed by the qayl of the tribe S¹mʿy.

Ja 616+Ja 622 depicts an expedition ordered by Ns²ʾkrb Yʾmn Yhrḥb, king of Sabaʾ and ḏu-Raydān, whose goal was to rescue and assist the tribe Ḫawlān Gudādān. The inscription doesn't make clear why exactly did the Ḫawlān Gudādān require Sabaean assistance. The Ḫawlān Gudādān then in thurn assisted the Sabaean army in their battle with the tribe of Dwʾt in the valleys of Bʾrn, Ḫlb and Tdḥn.

Ja 658+Ja 659 describes how the king of Sabaʾ, ḏu-Raydān, the Ḥaḍramawt and Ymnt, S²mr Yhrʿs², sent his army to protect the town of Ṣʿdtm and to make a peace settlement with Ḫawlān Gudādān. The text doesn't mention which side was responsible for the hostilities between Sabaʾ and Ḫawlān.

Ja 788+671 is a fragmentary inscription whose authors name cannot be determined. He was a qayl of Yrs¹m and ḏ-S¹mʿy and belonged to Ḫawlān Gudādān; he was sent by two Sabaean kings, Ṯʾrn Yhnʿm and his son Mlkkrb Yʾmn, to control the water wich had broken out when the dam in Ḥbbḍ and Rḥbm was destroyed. He managed to control the flood and to repair the dam in three months' time.

Robin-Umm Laylā 1 is a legal text which marks an assembly of the tribe Ḫawlān Gudādān and their allies. All the tribes agreed to defend their land against Ethiopian agression. The inscription near the end mentions the kings of Sabaʾ and the tribe of Sḫymm as the lords of Ḫawlān Gudādān.

Ja 601 and Nāmī NAG 7 relate the defeat inflicted upon Ḫawlan in the land of Ḫawlān Gudādān by the Sabaean king Wtrm Yhʾmn in two military expeditions as reprisal for certain offences commited by Ḫawlan against Sabaʾ which aren't mentioned in these texts.

Ja 616+Ja 622 describes a military expedition conducted by the Sabaean army during the reign of Ns²ʾkrb Yʾmn Yhrḥb, resulting in the submission of the tribe of H̱awlān Gudādān, whose free men were taken by the Sabaean army as hostages.

CIH 537+RES 4919 is a fragmentary construction text which marks the construction of the house Rymn. Since so many parts of the inscription are missing, it's impossible to tell what part did the tribe H̱awlān Gudādān take in this event.

The following inscriptions, which constitute the majority of inscriptions which mention the tribe H̱awlān, mention it without a compound name.

RES 3946 is the earliest inscription where the tribe of H̱awlan is attested. It is a text which commemorates how Krbʾl Wtr, son Ḏmrʿly mkrb of Sabaʾ, purchased a number of territories and possessions, among which was Gbrm, which had belonged to H̱awlan.

Ja 556 is a very short construction text which is dedicated to ʾlmqh for the completion of the wall upon which the inscription is written. The authors of the inscription are two administrative officials of the tribe H̱awlān.

CIH 140 chronicles one of the earliest wars between Saba' and the other South Arabian kingdoms, in this text specifically Qatabān, Ḥimyar, Ḥaḍramawt and Rdmn. It is therefore dated to the end of the 1st century and the beginning of the 2nd century CE. H̱awlan is mentioned as the land in which Saba' successfully fought the Ḥaḍramites.

CIH 220, RES 4137, BaBa al-Ḥadd 11 and BaBa al-Ḥadd 12 are very short fragmentary text which mention H̱awlan, but the inscriptions are completely indecipherable due to the level of damage they have sustained and therefore it is impossible to determine what was their purpose or what role the tribe H̱awlan in the events which these inscriptions were meant to commemorate. CIH 398 is another fragmentary text and is therefore difficult to fully understand; it is a dedicatory inscription authored by an author, perhaps Ṣdq son of ʿbdʿṯtr, written to express gratitude to ʾlmqh for a favor granted to the author of the inscription in the land of H̱awlan. What is certain is that the author was a subject of the Sabaean kings ʾls²rḥ Yḥḍb and his brother Yʾzl Byn.

BaBa al-Ḥadd 4, CIH 658, Ja 2864, Ja 2867 and MAFRAY-al-Maktūba 1 are construction texts which don't contain any information relevant to the political history of the tribe of Ḫawlan. They commemorate the completion of a number of construction projects performed under the authority of either Lḥy'ʿt Bryn or Lḥy'ʿṯt Yrḫm, both qayls of Radmān and Ḫawlan. Similarly, MAFRAY-ḏī-Ḥadīd 1, MAFRAY-ḏī-Ḥadīd 2, MAFRAY-Sāriʿ 6, RES 3958, RES 4100, Wādī Ḥarīr 1, YMN 10, YMN 13, YMN 14, YMN 3, YMN 4, YMN 9 and Dostal 1 are all construction texts, containing little relevant information regarding the political history of the tribe of Ḫawlan. For instance, MAFRAY-ḏī-Ḥadīd 1 narrates how a son of Mʿdkrb Yhmgd, the qayl of Radmān and Ḫawlan, completed a dike for his vineyard in the valley of Yfdʾb. The three inscriptions which do contain some relevant information are YMN 10, YMN 9 and Dostal 1. YMN 10 and YMN 9, which are dated to the year 144 and 146 of the Radmanite calendar respectively, which corresponds to 70 and 72 CE respectively, clearly indicate that the tribes Radmān and Ḫawlan were subjects of the king of Ḥaḍramawt, whereas Dostal 1 is a late inscription, dated to the year 566 of the Ḥimyarite calendar, which corresponds to 456 CE, and is one the rare inscriptions mentioning Ḫawlan which is clearly monotheistic.

MAFRAY-al-Miʿsāl 7 and MAFRAY-al-Miʿsāl 9 are two short and personal dedicatory inscriptions which contain little information regarding the political position of this tribe in South Arabia; they do, however, give us a glimpse into the more ordinary events in the lives of South Arabian nobility. Namely, MAFRAY-al-Miʿsāl 7 expresses gratitude of its author, S¹ydm ʾrs³l son of the qayl of Radmān and Ḫawlan, for killing his first panter, whereas MAFRAY-al-Miʿsāl 9 expresses gratitude of Mʿdkrb ʾs¹ʾr, also son of the qayl of Radmān and Ḫawlan, for killing his slave for undetermined reason.

CIH 308 commemorates three separate events; one is the completion of a large construction project by two Sabaean kings, ʿlhn Nhfn and Yrm ʾymn. The other is the alliance between the two Sabaean kings and Gdrt, the king of Aksum, which followed a similar alliance concluded between Sabaʾ and Ydʿʾb Ġyln, king of Ḥaḍramawt. The final event is the defeat inflicted upon Ḫawlan by the Sabaean army.

The subject of all of the following inscriptions is warfare. DAI Barʾān 2000-1 is a short inscription which chronicles a number of victories accomplished by S^2ʿrm ʾwtr king of Sabaʾ against a number of South Arabian tribes and kingdoms, Ḫawlan included among them.

Ir 12 chronicles how Wfym ʾḏrḥ, in service of the Sabaean king S^2ʿrm ʾwtr, performed garrison duty on the borders of the tribe Ḥs^2dm during the war with the Ethiopians and their allies the tribes of S^1whrn and Ḫawlan.

Ir 13 is a dedicatory inscription which gives a very lengthy account of a successful military campaign waged by the Sabaean king S^2ʿrm ʾwtr against the army of the king of Ḥaḍramawt, ʾlʿz Ylṭ, and his allies Ḫawlan, Qatabān, Radmān, Mḍḥy, as well as the tribes of Awsān, Qs^3mm and Ḥdlm. The victorious Sabaean army managed to annihilate this army and kill the son of the king of Ḥaḍramawt in his palace S^2qr, in the town of S^2bwt, and to rescue Mlkḥlk, the sister of S^2ʿrm ʾwtr.

Ja 649 is an account of a number of successful assaults performed by Wfym ʾḥbr in the service of the Sabaean king S^2mr Yhrʿs^2. One of these attacks he mounted alongside hundred and seventy members of the tribes of Ḫawlan and Ṣirwāḥ against the tribes of ʿAkk and ḏ-S^1hrtm at the fortress of Rgzgzn.

Sh 31 is a dedicatory text in which its author, Rymn ḏ-Ḥzfrm, expresses gratitude to ʾlmqh Ṯhwn for allowing him safe return from his two missions which he performed in service of the king of Saba', S^2mr Yhrʿs^2. The first was a diplomatic mission to Persia, and the second mission was performed for a period of forty years, during which Rymn ḏ-Ḥzfrm performed the role of governor in the land of Ḫawlan.

MAFRAY-al-Miʿsāl 2 is a dedicatory inscription written by Lḥyʿt ʾwkn, the qayl of Radmān and Ḫawlan, to express his gratitude for his safe return from the battle in the plain of Ḥurma, where he fought in the Ḥimyarite army in service of Krbʾl ʾyfʿ against the Sabaean king ʾls^2rḥ Yḥḍb. This battle took place, according to this inscription, in the year 363 of the Ḥimyarite calendar.

MAFRAY-al-Miʿsāl 4 narrates how a qayl of Radmān and Ḫawlan, Nṣrm Yhḥmd ibn Mʿhr and ḏ-Ḫwln, assisted with his army the king of Ḥaḍramawt, ʾlʿz Ylṭ, to quell the rebellion of tribes Yhbʾr, ḏ-Hgrm, Gdmm, Ṣdfn, ḏ-Ks³rn and Mahra. The army of Radmān and Ḫawlan helped lift the siege of the town of Šabwa, then assaulted and defeated the rebellious tribes at the town of Ṣwʾrn.

MAFRAY-al-Miʿsāl 5 is a long account of the military exploits of Ḥẓyn ʾwkn ibn Mʿhr and ḏ-Ḫwln, qayl of the tribe of Rdmn and Ḫawlan. He fought in the service of Ys¹rm Yhnʿm, king of Sabaʾ and ḏu-Raydān. Among the enemies defeated by the qayl of Rdmn and Ḫawlan were the Ethiopian army and their allies.

It is clear that the tribes of Ḫawlan were for the most part vassals of Ḥimyar, and fought alongside their army against their enemies.

1.7. Ḥimyar (*ḥmyr^m*)

Ḥimyar is the second most widely attested South Arabian tribe or polity analyzed in this thesis; they are mentioned in forty-two inscriptions.

Two of these inscriptions, CIAS 47.82/o 2 and CIAS 95.11/o 2 were written in Qatabānic, both dated to the D period. These inscriptions were ordered by two women, Gdnʿm and Ḥmdʿly, who, along with their children, invoke divine protection for the Qatabānian ruler Nbṭm Yhnʿm in his fight against Saba and Ḥimyar. One other inscription which wasn't written in Sabaic is RES 2687 (B2). It is a construction text written in Ḥaḍramitic, and it records the construction of the fortress of Qlt by Yashhurʾil Yhrʿs², mukarrib of Ḥaḍramawt, as protection against Ḥimyarite agression.

CIH 332 is a very short fragment of a dedicatory inscription. It is also the only inscription in this subchapter that isn't dated to any period. Ḥimyar is mentioned alongside Ḥaḍramawt, but because of the small size of the fragment, it is difficult to determine what the context was.

CIH 140 is the only inscription mentioning Ḥimyar that's written in Sabaic and dated to the C period. It is a dedicatory text which was written to commemorate success in the Sabaean war against Ḥimyar, Qatabān, Rdmn and Ḥaḍramawt during the reign of ʾls^2rḥ Yḥḍb.

BR-M. Bayḥān 1, like the majority of the inscriptions which follow, is dated to the D period. It is a dedicatory inscription which was erected by two royal officials of the Sabaean king ʾls^2r Yḥḍb as a sign of gratitude to ʾlmqh for success in battle against Ḥimyar in the plain of ḏ-Ḥrmtm which, according to the historical notes on the DASI web site, took place in 249 CE.

BR-M. Bayḥān 4 is also a dedicatory text which praises the military success of the Sabaean kingʾls^2rḥ Yḥḍb and his brother Yʾzl Byn against Ḥimyar, although, unlike BR-M. Bayḥān 1, this inscription doesn't give any details regarding the time or the location of the battle in question.

CIAS 39.11/o 1 n° 1 is a fragmentary inscription which is eroded and therefore difficult to fully decipher, but from the readable parts of the text it is clear that it is also a dedicatory inscription erected in gratitude to ʾlmqh for a victorious battle led by ʾls^2rḥ Yḥḍb against his Ḥimyarite enemies.

CIAS 39.11/o 2 n° 2 gives us more details about the military campaign led by ʾls^2rḥ Yḥḍb; this text states that the Sabaean kings, ʾls^2rḥ Yḥḍb and his brother Yzʾl Byn, defeated a Ḥimyarite king, probably Shammar Yuhahamid, and "armed forces of Ḥimyar" at the field of ḏ-Ḥrmtm and ʾẓwr, and that they conquered Ḥimyarite towns and fortresses.

CIAS 39.11/o 2 n° 3 is another in the line of texts celebrating Sabaean triumph over Ḥimyar, this time written from the point of view of two servants of ʾls^2rḥ Yḥḍb, Whbʾwm and S^1ʿdʾwm, who fought in the battle at the field of Ḥurmatum.

CIAS 39.11/o 3 n° 1 and CIAS 39.11/o 3 n° 5 are two dedicatory inscription which were erected by other participants in the Sabaean-Ḥimyarite war as a sign of gratitude for success in war and safe return from the land of Ḥimyar.

CIH 155 (c180-217 AD, based on the mention of Yd''b Ġyln, king of Ḥaḍramawt) is a fragmentary text which briefly mentions Ḥimyar as the target of a Sabaean assault in the fortress of ḏt-ʿrmn.

CIH 314+CIH 954 is an account of an Ethiopian diplomatic mission which was sent to ʾls²rḥ Yḥḍb and his brother Y'zl Byn to ask for peace with the kingdom of Saba'. The text mentions that Ḥimyar called the Ethiopians for help in their war with Saba'.

CIH 334 is a dedicatory text according to which the Ḥimyarites fought as allies on the side of S²ʿrm ʾwtr, king of Sabaʾ and ḏu-Raydān, who defeated Ḥaḍramawt.

CIH 343 doesn't contain much useful information regarding Ḥimyar, since it is an inscription in which a member of the tribe of S¹myʿm praises their patron deity Tʾlb-Rymm for, among other things, protecting his tribe from Ḥimyar.

CIH 347 is another inscription dedicated to Tʾlb Rymm in gratitude for protecting the author of the inscription when he took part in the war between Saba' and Ḥimyar.

CIH 350 gives us an account of successful military raids performed by members of the Ḥs²dm, who were, according to this text, under the vassalage of the tribe of Hamdān. The targets of these expeditions were, among others, Ḥimyar and the Ethiopians.

CIH 353 describes a Sabaean military expedition against Ḥimyar, apparently in the city of Ḍhr, where the Ḥimyarite army garrison was defeated.

FB-Maḥram Bilqīs 3 is a description of a successful Sabaean military campaign conducted against Ḥimyar during the reign of ʾls²rḥ Yḥḍb and his brother Yʾzl Byn.

Ir 32 is a lengthy account of the Ḥimyarite conquest of Ḥaḍramawt, listing a large number of cities which were conquered in this campaign.

Ir 69 describes how Ḥimyar sent a diplomatic mission to the Sabaean kings, ʾls²rḥ Yḥḍb and his brother Yʾzl Byn, which achieved peace and military alliance between Ḥimyar and Saba' against the Ethiopians. Ḥimyarite army assisted the Sabaean army in the battle against the Ethiopians in Mqrfm, in the land of ʿAkk, where the Ethiopians were defeated.

Ja 576+Ja 577 is a very lengthy inscription which chronicles the military campaign conducted by the two kings of Sabaʾ and ḏu-Raydān, ʾls^{2}rḥ Yḥḍb and his brother Yʾzl Byn. Their main enemies were the Ḥimyarites and their allies the Ethiopians, as well as any other tribe who were allied with them. According to the text, he Sabaean army managed to defeat their Ḥimyarite and Ethiopian enemies in every one of the numerous battles which they fought in this campaign.

Ja 578 is a detailed account of a battle, which is also described in MAFRAY-al-Miʿsāl 2, between the forces of Saba' and Ḥimyar in the reign of ʾls^{2}rḥ Yḥḍb and his brother Yʾzl Byn, where the Sabaean army was victorious. This is the first inscription in which the leader of Ḥimyar is mentioned by name, Krbʾl ḏu-Raydān. The fighting took place first in the field of Ḥurma, then in the wadi of ʾẓwr, after which the Ḥimyarite army was defeated and scattered.

Ja 579 mentions a Sabaean military raid against Ḥimyar and ḏ-S^{1}hrtm in the land of Ḥimyar and the city of Ngrn.

Ja 580 is a short dedicatory inscription which expresses gratitude of a steward of the Sabaean king ʾls^{2}rḥ Yḥḍb and his brother Yʾzl Byn because he safely returned from a military operation conducted in the land of Ḥimyar, without specifically mentioning the part of the Ḥimyarite land which was attacked.

Ja 581 similarly narrates a successful military campaign waged by a steward of the same two Sabaean kings against Ḥimyar

Ja 586 contains more details regarding the war waged by ʾls^{2}rḥ Yḥḍb and his brother Yʾzl Byn against Ḥimyar.

Ja 665 chronicles the Ḥimyarite conquest of Ḥaḍramawt.

Ja 740 is a dedicatory inscription which serves to express the gratitude of its author, Rbʾwm ʾṣdq, for his safe return from the military campaign performed in the land of Ḥimyar in the service of his tribe Sabaʾ.

Nāmī NAG 15 is very similar in that it expresses the gratitude of its author, Ns^{2}ʾkrb ḏ-Mḥltm, who conducted a military campaign in the land of Ḥimyar. This inscription is a bit different than most inscriptions which chronicle wars which the authors of the inscriptions wish to commemorate in that Nāmī NAG 15 doesn't name the king who ordered the military campaign mentioned in the text, but his successor who became the ruler the year after the war had ended, and his name was Whbʾl Yḥz.

Ry 548 is similarly authored by a servant of the Sabaean kings who returned safely from a military expedition in Ḥimyar. The kings who ordered this expedition were ʾls^{2}rḥ Yḥḍb and his brother Yʾzl Byn.

YM 18307 is a fragmentary text which, although a large part of it is missing, clearly serves as a dedicatory inscription to the successful military campaign against Ḥimyar. Its author is the king who conducted this campaign, Rbs^{2}ms^{1}m Nmrn.

MAFRAY-al-Miʿsāl 2 (179 Radm=363 Ḥim) narrates the battle between the armies of Ḥimyar and Sabaʾ in the plain of Ḥurma. This inscription claims that the Ḥimyarite army, under the command of Krbʾl ʾyfʿ, was victorious, whereas Ja 578, which was written by two *qayls* who fought in the Sabaean army, claims victory for Sabaʾ.

MAFRAY-al-Miʿsāl 5 (198 Radm) is a long chronicle of a series of victorious military campaigns conducted by the qyl of the tribes of Rdmn and Ḫwln in the service of Ys^{1}rm Yhnʿm, king of Sabaʾ and ḏu-Raydān. The land of Ḥimyar is mentioned as one of the targets of these campaigns, specifically because of the presence of the Ethiopian army there.

Quṣayr 1 is a construction text which is badly damaged at places. It marks the damage that was done to the irrigation systems by the armies of Ḥaḍramawt, Qatabān, Sabaʾ, Ms^{2}rqn and Ḥimyar during their wars, as well as the repairs done by the members of the tribe Yashmar.

The following inscriptions are dated to the E period, and most of them mention the year in which they were written. CIH 540 is a detailed construction text which describes how S^{2}rḥbʾl Yʿfr king of Sabaʾ, ḏu-Raydān, Ḥaḍramawt and Ymnt repaired the dam (at Marib) which had been destroyed by spring floods, and the members of Ḥimyar and Ḥaḍramawt were called upon to perform these construction works. The text dates this event to the year 565 according to the Ḥimyarite calendar.

Gar Sharahbil A and Gar Sharahbil B, are construction texts which are authored by S²rḥb'l Y'fr, king of Saba', ḏu-Raydān, Ḥaḍramawt, Yamanat and the Bedouins of Ṭwdm and of Thmt in the year 572 of the Ḥimyarite calendar. They mark, among other construction works, the repair of the dam of Ma'rib.

Ry 510, dated to the year 631 of the Ḥimyarite calendar, is a short dedicatory inscription. Its subject is a military expedition conducted by M'dkrb Y'fr, king of Saba', ḏu-Raydān, Ḥaḍramawt, Yamanat, and the Bedouin of Ṭwdm and of Thmt, against the rebellious Bedouins in the plain of Kt'.

CIH 621 marks one of the turning points in South Arabian history, as it commemorates the repair works done by the tribe of Yz'n in the year 640 of the Ḥimyarite calendar, remarking how these works were performed after the Ethiopian army entered Ḥimyarite land and killed the king of Ḥimyar.

CIH 541, dated to the year 658 of the Ḥimyarite calendar, is likewise a very long and detailed construction inscription. Unlike CIH 540, however, this text is Christian, since it is authored by the Ethiopian king Abraha, who expresses his gratitude to Rḥmnn, the Messiah and the Holy Ghost.

Finally, Ist 7608 bis is a fragmentary dedicatory inscription, and therefore some of the information in the text is unclear. Its subject seems to be the appointment of governors from the tribe of Yz'n by the Ethiopian king 'l'ṣbḥh, also known as king Kaleb of Aksum, to maintain order in the land of Ḥimyar. The text is also written by a Christian, as it expresses gratitude to Rḥmnn and his son Christ.

1.8. Kinda (*kdt*)

The tribe of Kinda (*Kdt*) is attested in fourteen inscriptions, although one of them, the inscription Ph-Ry-Li, contains only the name of a Kindite ruler while the rest of it is virtually unreadable and is therefore of little use. The inscriptions CIAS 39.11/o 2 n° 8, Ja 660 and ʿAbadān 1 also contain little relevant information. CIAS 39.11/o 2 n° 8 is a dedicatory text which only mentions that a Sabaean king embarked on a mission to kingdoms north of Sabaʾ, Kinda being one of them. Ja 660 describes a military campaign conducted by S^{2}mr Yhrʿs^2, king of Sabaʾ, ḏu-Raydān, Ḥaḍramawt and Ymnt, against the tribes of Nḫʿn and Grm; Kinda is only mentioned at the beginning of the inscription, and its role in these events, as described by this text, is unclear. ʿAbadān 1 gives us a lengthy account of the Ḥimyarite conquests; the role of Kinda in these wars is unclear in this text, however, as this inscription only mentions Kinda once, in an incomplete sentence.

The next five inscriptions are dated to the D period. Ja 635 is a dedicatory text which commemorates the successful run of military campaigns conducted by ʾbkrb ʾḥrs^1, in service of S^{2}ʿrm ʾwtr, king of Sabaʾ and ḏu-Raydān. According to the text, he led two successful military operations against Rbʿt, king of Kinda and Qḥṭn.

DAI Barʾān 2000-1 is a dedicatory inscription which chronicles a military campaign by S^{2}ʿrm ʾwtr king of Sabaʾ and ḏu Raydān against a number of tribes, Kinda included among them. The text mentions that Rbʿt bn Mʿwyt, king of Kinda and Qaḥṭān, was made prisoner and brought as a captive to Ṣanʿāʾ.

The inscriptions Ir 32 and Ja 665 were written by the same author, S^{1}ʿdtʾlb Ytlf, who is identified as the kbr of the Arabs of the king of Sabaʾ, Kinda, Mḏḥgm, Ḥrmm, Bhlm and Zydʾl. Both texts chronicle the Ḥimyarite conquest of Ḥaḍramawt and the role of the "Arabs of Kinda" in them, and they appear to have been Ḥimyarite subjects rather than allies.

Ja 576+Ja 577 is a very long inscription, which chronicles a number of military campaigns conducted by ʾls^{2}rḥ Yḥḍb, king of Sabaʾ and ḏu Raydan. The text claims that ʾls^{2}rḥ Yḥḍb succeeded in his war against Kinda and that he managed to imprison Mlkm, king of Kinda, and forced him to give ʾls^{2}rḥ Yḥḍb horses and camels as reparations.

Ry 510, like all of the following inscriptions, is dated to the E period. It mentions Kinda as an ally of M'dkrb Y'fr, king of Saba', ḏu-Raydān, Ḥaḍramawt and Yamanat, whom they assisted in his expedition against the tribe of Mḏrm. The inscription is dated to the year 631 of the Ḥimyarite calendar, which corresponds to 521 CE.

Ry 509 describes the campaign of 'bkrb 's[1]'d and his son Ḥs[3]n Yh'mn, kings of Saba', ḏu-Raydān, Ḥaḍramawt and Yamanat, against the tribe of Ma'add (M'dm). Kinda is mentioned here as an ally of these two kings.

The inscriptions Ja 1028, Ry 507, and Ry 508, give us an account of the exploits of the Jewish ruler Yws[1]f 's[1]'r Yṯ'r, also known as ḏu-Nuwas, against the Christian kingdoms in South Arabia; the most notorious of these events being the siege of Nağrān and the destruction of the church in Zafar. Ja 1028 is dated to the year 633 of the Ḥimyarite era, which corresponds to 523 CE, Ry 507 was written in July of the same year, while Ry 508 was written in August. The tribe of Kinda is mentioned in both Ja 1028 and Ry 508 as an ally of Yws[1]f 's[1]'r Yṯ'r , whom the Kindites assisted in the siege of Nağrān. In contrast to Ry 506, the inscription Ja 1028 is explicitly Jewish, praising the rb-Hd (the lord of the Jews), whereas Ry 508 gives a more generally monotheistic praise to Rḥmnn.

The inscription Ry 506 records Abraha's campaign against the rebellious tribe of Bny 'mrm, as well as his assault on the tribe of Ma'add. This inscription is dated to the year 662 of the Ḥimyarite era, which corresponds to 552 CE. Kinda is mentioned as Abraha's ally in his subjugation of the Bny 'mrm. The author of this inscription invokes the God Rḥmnn and his Messiah (Rḥmnn w-ms[1]ḥ-hw) at the beginning.

Based on these inscriptions, it seems that the tribe of Kinda had been subjugated by Saba' and served it as vassals, but later on changed their allegiance and became allies of the Ethiopians.

1.9. Maḏḥiğ (*mḏḥg^m*)

The tribe of Maḏḥiğ is mentioned in nine inscriptions. The shortest of them, Bāfaqīh AF 1, doesn't contain much useful information; its author dedicates the text to ḏ-Smwy, the Lord of Yġrw, which he promise to do when he was on an expedition to the land of Maḏḥiğ.

CIAS 39.11/o 2 n° 8 (D) doesn't contain useful information regarding the political role and importance of this tribe in ancient South Arabia, only mentions that a Sabaean king embarked on a mission to kingdoms north of Saba, and Maḏḥiğ is mentioned as one of them. The inscription Ry 510 (E, 631 Ḥim) gives us a short account of a military expedition of Mʿdkrb Yʿfr, whom the Maḏḥiğ served as allies.

As it was already mentioned in the subchapter whose subject is the tribe of Kinda, the inscriptions Ja 1028, and Ry 508 (E, 633 Ḥim) chronicle the military expeditions conducted by Ḏū Nuwās against the Christian South Arabian kingdoms. Maḏḥiğ is mentioned alongside Kinda as one of the tribes who supported Ḏū Nuwās in his assault on Nağrān. According to the inscription Ja 1028, Maḏḥiğ was part of the army which guarded the coast against Ethiopian attack.

In the inscriptions Ir 32 (D) and Ja 665 (D), the tribe of Maḏḥiğ is only mentioned as part of the royal title of S¹ʿdtʾlb Ytlf, kbr of the Arabs of the king of Sabaʾ, Kinda, Mḏḥgm, Ḥrmm, Bhlm and Zydʾl. In Ja 660 (D) the role of Maḏḥiğ in this text isn't entirely clear, although it seems clear that it is also mentioned as part of a royal title.

Maḏḥiğ is mentioned in the ʿAbadān 1 (D, 470 Ḥim) inscription once, but the sentence is incomplete, which makes the role of Maḏḥiğ in the events chronicled in this text, namely the military expeditions performed by noblemen of the tribes Yzʾn, Ms²rqn and Ḍyftn, unclear.

Based on these inscriptions, the power and role that the tribe of Maḏḥiğ played in ancient South Arabia cannot be accurately determined, but the fact that they are mentioned in a small number of inscriptions, and that the name of Maḏḥiğ is mentioned as a part of a royal title, indicate that they could not have played a major role in pre-Islamic South Arabia.

1.10. Mahra (*mhrt*)

The tribe of Mahra is attested in three inscriptions. The shortest of the three, MAFYS-Ḍura᾽ 3, is a construction text which marks the repair of the irrigation system of S¹hbm, performed under the authority of a number of tribal leaders. Mahra are mentioned as one the tribes whose qayl repaired the system which was damaged by flood.

The inscription MAFRAY-al-Mi῾sāl 4 (E, 598 Ḥim, which corresponds to 488 CE) mentions Mahra as one of the tribes who were a part of the military expedition conducted by Nṣrm Yhḥmd, the *qayl* of Rdmn.

The longest inscription is ῾Abadān 1 (D, 470 Ḥim, which corresponds to 360 CE), which chronicles a large number of military expeditions performed by noblemen of the tribes Yz᾽n, Ms²rqn and Ḍyftn. Even though the role of Mahra in these events isn't entirely clear because the text is at places unreadable, it appears that Mahra were among the targets of these expeditions. Based on the small number of inscriptions which mention the name of Mahra, it seems that this tribe played a minor role in ancient South Arabia.

1.11. Murād

This South Arabian tribe was a part of the tribal group of Maḏḥiǧ.[260]The Murād resided in the territory of al-Ǧawf, east of Naǧrān and Ma᾽rib.[261]

It is attested in three inscriptions, ῾Abadān 1, Ja 1028 and Ry 506. In ῾Abadān 1, Murād are listed among the tribes which took part in the Ḥimyarite conquest in central and south Arabia, although their exact role in these events isn't clear. Ja 1028 narrates the campaign conducted by king Yws¹f ᾽s¹᾽r Yṯ᾽r against South Arabian Christians. The tribe of Murād took part in this campaign alongside Hamdān, helping them guard the coast against

---

260 EI³, s.v. Murād (M. Aathar Ali).
261 Ibid.

Ethiopian forces. Ry 506 is a chronicle of the Ḥimyarite king ʾAbraha's military campaign in central Arabia. Murād are listed among his allies or vassals who took part in the battle against the tribe of Maʿadd. After Maʿadd had surrendered, ʾAbraha appointed the son of the defeated leader of Maʿadd as their new chief.

2. MEDIEVAL HISTORICAL SOURCES

2.1. HISTORY

The process of Islamization of South Arabia is difficult to analyze due to the lack of contemporary sources. The later sources, such as al-Ṭabarī's history, offer sparse information regarding this issue. According to him, the Islamization of South Arabia started with Bāḏām^{n}, one of the *Abnā*ʾ[262] and the ruler of Ṣanʿāʾ.[263] Following the conversion of Bāḏām^{n} and the *Abnā*ʾ to Islam, Muḥammad sent his representatives to South Arabian tribes, however the role of these representatives is unclear.[264]

These representatives may be divided into two groups, religious teachers and judges on the one hand and certain tribal leaders who had already adopted Islam on the other.[265] It is possible that these were meant to work together; the Islamic teachers were to spread the faith while the South Arabian tribal leaders were to enforce their authority and assist them politically in the conversion to Islam. [266]

The situation changed quickly after Muḥammad's death in the year 11 according to Hiğra i.e. 632 CE. His death caused a crisis of succession; on the same day that Muḥammad died, Abū Bakr, one of Muḥammad's earliest and closest associates, was proclaimed the first caliph, i.e. successor to Muḥammad. This proclamation wasn't universally accepted within the Muslim community however. Many tribes throughout the Arabian Peninsula refused to continue paying taxes to the central authorities in Medina, which led to the wars which are known by Islamic historiography as the Wars of Apostasy; namely, Abū Bakr insisted that all

---

262 Abnāʾ were the descendants of Persians who ruled Yemen. cf. EI^{3}, s.v. al-Abnāʾ (K. V. Zettersteen)

263 Al-Ṭabarī: *Tārīḫ al-Umam wa-l-Mulūk*, p. 495

264 EI^{3}, s.v. al-Yaman (G.R. Smith).

265 Al-Medej: *Yemeni relations*, p. 33

266 Ibid.

the tribes which had accepted Islam and paid taxes to Medina during Muḥammad's reign were obligated to continue doing so.[267]

The traditional view within Islamic historiography was that Muḥammad managed to convert entire Arabia to Islam, and when these tribes revolted after his death, they also revolted from Islam and reverted to polytheism, which led Abū Bakr to wage against in order to bring them back to Islam. The first campaign within the Wars of Apostasy targeted the tribes Ġaṭafān, Tayyi'i and ʾAsad, which were located north-east of Medina. Following their defeat, the Muslim army advanced toward al-Yamāma, Baḥrayn, defeating all the rebellious tribes along the way[268].

South Arabia was an exception, however, since the first rebellion against Medina began before Muḥammad's death. This rebellion was lead by ʿAbhala bin Kaʿb of ʿAns, also known as al-ʾAswad, who was not only a political but also a religious rebel since he claimed to be a prophet[269]. He received support among his own tribe of ʿAns, as well as various branches of Maḏḥiğ. also he formed his army in Nağrān, and used this army to defeat the ʾAbnāʾ in Ṣanʿāʾ, led by Bāḏām's son Šahr, and take control of Ṣanʿāʾ[270]. While it is certain that this rebellion was supported by numerous tribes, it is difficult to say whether his direct rule extended further that Ṣanʿāʾ, his takeover of Ṣanʿāʾ forced Muḥammad's representatives to flee Ṣanʿāʾ.[271]

His rule was short-lived, however, since he was soon assassinated by a group of his close associates. The participants of the conspiracy were Qays and members of the ʾAbnāʾ. However, after the death of al-Aswad, the conflict between Qays and ʾAbnāʾ took place.[272] The relations between conspirators with each other and with Muḥammad is described differently in sources. On the one hand, in Balaḏuri's version of the story, Qays had the key role in the conspiracy; he was sent by Muḥammad to fight al-Aswad. Finally, he killed al-

---

267 Ellias Shoufani: *Al-Riddah and the Muslim conquest of Arabia.* Toronto: University of Toronto Press, 1973, pp. 1-2.
268 Ibid., p.5.
269 Ibid., p.7-8.
270 Ibid., p.90.
271 Ibid.
272 Ibid. p. 91.

Aswad with the help of ʾAbnā[273]. However, according to Sayf b. ʿUmar, the ʾAbnā had the key role in these events[274]. The ʾAbnā organized the conspiracy under the request of Muḥammad.

Shoufani explains that this event from the point of view of political relations; according to him, the problem of division of power was behind the conspiracy[275]. None of the three political forces in the field were strong enough to defeat each other. Therefore, initially Qays and the ʾAbnāʾ behaved as allies in order to defeat al-Aswad, bu after his death they fought among each other for political power[276]. In response to these events, Abū Bakr sent al-Muhāğir b. ʾAbī ʾUmayya to Yemen, and he managed to subdue Qays and finally make South Arabia part of the Islamic caliphate[277]

2.1.1 al-ʾAšʿar

The tribe of al-ʾAšʿar is mentoned in aṭ-Ṭabarī's history for the first time in his account of the battle at Ḫunayn. This battle took place in the 8th year according to Hiğra, which corresponds to 629-630 CE. This battle was fought between an army composed of north Arabian tribes Hawāzin, Ṯaqīf, Naṣr, Ğušam and Hilāl on one side, and the Muslim adhurirmy on the other. According to al-Ṭabarī, members of al-ʾAšʿar took part in this battle on Muḥammad's side, and one of them, Abu ʾAmīr al-ʾAšʿarī, was martyred.[278]

When Muḥammad returned to Medina after his final pilgrimage, he appointed a number of men who were to govern South Arabia. He appointed a man named aṭ-Ṭāhir bin ʾAbī Hāla to govern the two tribes of al-ʾAšʿar and ʿAkk. They were the first south Arabian tribes to rebel following the death of Muḥammad, alongside the tribe of ʿAkk. The governor

---

273 Ibid. p. 92.
274 Ibid. p. 93.
275 Ibid., 95.
276 Ibid.
277 Al-Medej: *Yemeni relations*, p.75.
278 Al-Ṭabarī: *Tārīḫ al-Umam wa-l-Mulūk*, pp. 440-444

appointed by Muḥammad, aṭ-Ṭāhir bin ʾAbī Hāla, led an army with which he assaulted and routed the rebellious tribesmen on the coastal road on al-Aʾlab. [279]

2.1.2 ʿAkk

After the death of Bāḏām, the tribe of ʿAkk was placed under the same governor as the tribe of al-ʾAšʿar, aṭ-Ṭāhir bin ʾAbī Hāla.[280]

ʿAkk were the first to rebel in the Tihāma after Muḥammad's death alongside the tribe of al-ʾAšʿar.When Muḥammad returned to Medina after his final pilgrimage, he appointed a number of men who were to govern South Arabia. He appointed a man named aṭ-Ṭāhir bin ʾAbī Hāla to govern the two tribes of al-ʾAšʿar and ʿAkk. They were the first south Arabian tribes to rebel following the death of Muḥammad, alongside the tribe of ʿAkk. The governor appointed by Muḥammad, aṭ-Ṭāhir bin ʾAbī Hāla, led an army with which he assaulted and routed the rebellious tribesmen on the coastal road on al-Aʾlab. He had informed Abū Bakr of his intentions to fight these two tribes, and once he had achieved victory at al-Aʾlab, he received a response from Abū Bakr praising his decision and ordering him to occupy the road on al-A`lab until he received further insctructions.[281]

During the second rebellion in South Arabia, the tribe of ʿAkk was on the side of the Muslim army. Fayrūz, who belonged to ʾAbnāʾ and was the ally of Abū Bakr[282], sent a message to them, asking for their assistance, and warriors of ʿAkk defended the families of the ʾAbnāʾ, as well as sending reinforcements to Fayrūz's army which helped him in the battle against Qays at Ṣanʿāʾ.[283]

---

279 Ibid, p. 495
280 Ibid.
281 Ibid., 525
282 Ibid., 526
283 Ibid

During the wars of the Islamic conquests, members of this tribe played a prominent role in the conquest of Egypt.[284]

2.1.3 Ǧarm

The tribe of Ǧarm itself isn't mentioned in the account regarding the Wars of Apostasy. However, two branches of this tribe, Banū Nāǧiyya and Rasīb, which had migrated to ʿUmān before the appearance of Islam[285], did play a role in these events. After Muḥammad's death, the people of ʿUmān and the tribe of Mahra rebelled against Medina under the leadership of Laqīṭ bin Malik al-ʾAzdī, who proclaimed himself prophet. The two branches of Ǧarm assisted the Muslim army which was dispatched to combat the rebels; Banū Nāǧiyya sent reinforcements which helped the Muslim army achieve victory over Laqīṭ in the battle in the town of Ḍabāʾ. This army was later joined by reinforcements from Rasīb and a number of ʿUmāni tribes in the victorious campaign against the Mahra rebels. [286]

2.1.4. Hamdān

After Muḥammad returned from his military expedition in Tabūk, he received a letter from Ḥimyarite rulers announcing their acceptance of Islam. Among them was al-Nu'man, the prince of Ḏū Ruʿayn, Hamdān, and al-Maʿāfir.[287]

When Muḥammad returned to Medina after his final pilgrimage, he appointed a number of men who were to govern south Arabia. He appointed a man named ʾAmīr b. Shahr to govern the Hamdān around 632 CE.[288]

---

284 EI^3, s.v. ʿAkk (W. Gaskell).
285 The History of al- Ṭabarī . *Volume* X. The Conquest of Arabia, trans. Fred M. Donner, p. 154, note 966
286 Al-Ṭabarī: *Tārīḫ al-Umam wa-l-Mulūk*, p. 523
287 Ibid. p. 457

During the episode with al-ʿAnsī, Qays had a number of warriors from the Hamdān and Ḥimyar in his entourage who assisted him in killing al-ʿAnsī.[289]

Considering the fact that the tribe of Hamdān didn't revolt either during the first rebellion of al-ʾAswad al-ʿAnsī nor after Muḥammad's death, it seems that the tribe as a whole remained loyal to Medina. During the wars of the Islamic conquest parts of Hamdān remained in the Yemen and parts became dispersed in the conquered territories, a large group of them had settled at Kūfa and were supporters of ʻAlī ibn Abī Ṭālib.[290]

2.1.5 Ḫawlān

The deputation of Ḫawlān arrived in Mecca in the year 10 according to Hiğra, announcing their acceptance of Islam.[291]

Qays led a second revolt against the ʾAbnāʾ in South Arabia; he first killed Dadhawayh and then attempted to kill Fayrūs, who eluded him and fled to his maternal relatives, the Ḫawlān tribe. From here, he informed Abū Bakr of the new rebellion and rallied loyal tribesmen from a central Arabia tribe Banu ʿUqayl b. Rabīʿa b. ʾAmīr b. Ṣaʿṣaʿ as well as from ʻAkk to assist him. [292]

Based on this information, it seems that the tribe of Ḫawlān did not take active part either in the rebellions against Medina, and that they provided refuge to Fayrus, the appointed governor, Ḫawlān clearly remained loyal to the Islamic state throughout this period.

2.1.6. Ḥimyar

---

288 Ibid. p. 495
289 Ibid., pp. 27-28, 497.
290 EI^3, s.v. Hamdān (J. Schleifer).
291 Al-Ṭabarī: *Tārīḫ al-Umam wa-l-Mulūk*, p. 464
292 Ibid., pp. 166-167.

After his military expedition against the Byzantines at Tabūk, the prophet Muḥammad received a number of delegations from various Arabian tribes and polities, announcing their acceptance of Islam. Among them, he received a letter sent by the kings of Ḥimyar al-Ḥāriṯ bin ʿAbd al-Kulāl, Nuʿaym bin ʿAbd al-Kulāl, and al-Nuʿmān, prince of Ḏū Ruʿayn, Hamdān, and Maʿāfir. Muḥammad responded by sending them a letter, in which he praised their conversion and informed them of their new obligations to Medina. [293]

The next episode in which the name Ḥimyar appears in aṭ-Ṭabarī history is the death of al-ʾAswad al-ʿAnsī, when an undisclosed number of members of the tribes of Hamdān and Ḥimyar assisted Qays in killing him.[294]

When Laqīṭ bin Malik al-ʾAzdī began his rebellion in ʿUmān, he forced the governors appointed by Muḥammad, Ǧayfar and ʿAbbād, to flee. Ǧayfar informed Abū Bakr of the rebellion, and Abū Bakr an army led by two men, Ḥuḏayfa bin Miḥṣan al-Ġalfānī of Ḥimyar to ʿUmān and ʿArfağa bin Harṯama al-Bāriqī of the ʾAzd to Mahra. Abū Bakr ordered them to work in unison and to begin crushing the rebellion in `Uman, with Ḥuḏayfa over ʿArfağa in ʿUmān, and ʿArfağa over Ḥuḏayfa in Mahra. They were assisted in this campaign by an army led by ʿIkrima, who had been previously sent to al-Yamama in central Arabia to suppress the uprising there but didn't succeed. This army managed to defeat Laqīṭ, and Ḥuḏayfa stayed in ʿUmān to maintain order.[295]

Based on these few instances of Ḥimyarite tribesmen in these events, the tribe seems to have remained loyal to the new Islamic state throughout the period of rebellions and its members assisted Abū Bakr in quelling these rebellions.

---

293 Ibid., pp. 73-74.

294 Al-Ṭabarī: *Tārīḫ al-Umam wa-l-Mulūk,* p. 497

295 Ibid., p. 152.

2.1.7. Kinda

During Muḥammad's expedition against Tabuk, his army reached an oasis called Dūma al-Ğandal, which was ruled by a Christian ruler of Kindite origin called ʾUkaydir bin ʿAbd al-Malik. He was forced to accept a peace agreement with Medina, under which he was obligated to pay tax to the Islamic state.[296]

After his return from this expedition, Muḥammad received delegations of various Arabian polities, pledging their allegiance to Medina and conversion to Islam. One of such delegations came from Kinda, and it was led by al-ʾAšʿa<u>t</u> bin Qays al-Kindī. During their conversation, he claimed that Muḥammad was a Kindite descendant, but Muḥammad rejected this claim.[297] Muḥammad did, however, attempt to marry a woman named Ġaziya bint Ğābir, who was from Kinda and who was renowned for her beauty. She refused the offer, however, and was allowed to return to her people. [298]

After Bāḏām's death, Muḥammad arranged the governance of South Arabia and appointed a governor over each tribe. The governor ʿUkāša bin Ṯawr bin Aṣġar al-Ġawṯī was appointed to govern three tribes, Sakāsīk, Sakūn, and Muʿāwiyya bin Kinda, which were branches of Kinda. [299]

Kinda, however, did not remain loyal to the Islamic state. Their rebellion came about due to a conflict which was caused by a dispute regarding the payment of taxes to Medina. The Muslim army did not immediately confront the rebels however, as the appointed governor Muhāğir hadn't yet assumed his post when the rebellion broke out. [300]

The cause of the rebellion of Kinda was a dispute between them and Ḥaḍramawt regarding the payment of taxes to Medina. The dispute led the Kinda to openly refuse to pay their taxes. The Muslim army was led by Ziyad and Muhāğir, and they forced the Kindite army to flee to an old fortress Nuğayr, were they were besieged by the Muslims. The fortress

---

296 Al-Ṭabarī: *Tārīḫ al-Umam wa-l-Mulūk*, p.454
297 Ibid., p. 97.
298 Ibid., pp. 136-137.
299 Ibid., p. 495
300 Ibid., p. 175

was surrounded from three sides, and the Muslim army managed to storm the fortress and destroy the Kindite army. [301]

This defeat was so devastating that apparently ʿUmar ibn Al-Ḫattāb, when he succeeded Abu Bakr as the caliph and decided to allow all Arabs who rebelled and were captured to be ransomed, the amount of ransom required to free a member of Kinda was lowered due to the heavy losses the tribe had suffered. This indicates that the power of this tribe was significantly lower compared to the status they had enjoyed in the pre-Islamic era.[302]

2.1.8. Maḏḥiǧ

Maḏḥiǧ were the first tribe to rebel after Muḥammad's final pilgrimage. They were led by Ḏū-l-Ḫimār ʿAbhala al-Kaʿbī, known as al-ʾAswad al-ʿAnsī. He deposed the governors appointed over Naǧrān. Not all members of Maḏḥiǧ followed him, though, as some of them joined Farwah b. Musayk, who had been appointed governor over Murād, a branch of Maḏḥiǧ. Farwah was deposed by Qays b. ʿAbd Yaġūṯ al-Murādī, of the clan Murād, a branch of Maḏḥiǧ, who was one of al-ʿAnsī's commanders during his reign. Farwah was the one who informed Muḥammad of the rebellion in Yemen.[303] Qays didn't remain loyal to al-ʿAnsī for long, however, and he was among the group of people who killed al-ʿAnsī. A group of tribesmen from Maḏḥiǧ and Hamdān were with Qays when al-ʿAnsī was killed.[304]

After al-ʾAswad al-ʿAnsī's death, and shortly before the death of Muḥammad, a delegation of al-Naḫa' came to Muḥammad, announcing their acceptance of Islam. They were the last Arabian tribe which sent a delegation to Muḥammad before his death.[305]

301 Ibid.
302 Ibid.
303 Ibid,. p. 480
304 Ibid., p. 28.
305 Ibid., p. 39.

2.1.9. Mahra

Mahra was one of the South Arabian tribes which rebelled after Muḥammad's death. When the Arabian tribes rebelled following Muḥammad's death, Abū Bakr organized the Muslim army in eleven groups, ordering them to go to various parts of Arabia and quell the rebellion. He ordered Huḏayfa b. Miḥṣan al-Ġalfāni to go to ʿUmān and he ordered ʿArfağa bin Harṯama to go towards Mahra, and he commanded them to cooperate, each one of being superior in his designated area over the other. Among these leaders was also ʿIkrima bin ʾAbī Ğahl, who was ordered to defeat Musaylima.[306] Musaylima confronted to Muḥammad, declaring himself a prophet, and led resistance of his tribe (Banū Ḥanīfa) in Ridda Wars[307].

ʿIkrima bin ʾAbī Ğahl suffered defeat, however, and was ordered by Abū Bakr to assist Huḏayfa and ʿArfağa in their assault on ʿUmān and Mahra. [308]

After the combined army of ʿIkrima, ʿArfağa and Huḏayfa defeated the rebels in ʿUmān, ʿIkrima continued his campaign against Mahra, assisted by tribesmen from ʿUmān. Once he reached Mahra territory, he encountered two subgroups of that tribe which were disunited and led by two different leaders. The first of them was led by Šaḫrit, who was a member of the tribe of Šakrat; the other group was larger and led by al-Muṣabbaḥ, a member of the tribe of Muḥārib. These two forces were in disagreement, because both leaders desired to command the other group. [309]

ʿIkrima exploited this disagreement by inviting the smaller force, which was following Šaḫrit, to return to Islam, which they accepted. ʿIkrima offered the same proposal to al-Muṣabbaḥ, but he refused. The united forces under ʿIkrima and Šaḫrit marched against al-Muṣabbaḥ, who was killed in the battle and his army was defeated. After the battle ʿIqrima sent a fifth of the booty with Šaḫrit to Abū Bakr, and divided the remaining booty among his army. This victory proved to be the end of the rebellion in Mahra, as they all embraced Islam and fought for ʿIkrima as he continued in his campaign towards Yemen.[310]

---

306 Ibid., p. 54.
307 EI^3, s.v. Musaylima (W. Montgomery Watt).
308 Al-Ṭabarī: *Tārīḫ al-Umam wa-l-Mulūk,* p. 105.
309 Ibid., p. 155.
310 Ibid.

2.2. THE AFTERMATH OF THE WARS OF APOSTASY

The wars of apostasy left were the last attempt by various South Arabian tribes and polities to win a certain level of autonomy, if not independence from the Islamic caliphate. Some of them led the rebellion, while others immediately took the side of the caliphate, whereas others were too insignificant to play an important role one way or the other.

ʿAkk fought as an ally of the Ethiopian army in the pre-Islamic period, and were ultimately conquered by Ḥimyar. During the wars of apostasy, they were the first to rebel against the authority of Medina, but after they were subjugated by the Muslim army, they fought as their allies against other South Arabian rebels.

Al-Ašʿar was an unimportant tribe in the pre-Islamic era, however, when Muḥammad died, they were the first to rebel, alongside ʿAkk. Their rebellion was unsuccessful, and they were quickly subjugated by the Islamic state.

The tribe of Ǧarm did not an important role in pre-Islamic South Arabia, as attested by the fact that there is only one inscription whichi mentions their name. The tribe itself did not play a role in the wars of apostasy either, but two branches of this tribe, Banū Nāǧiyya and Rasīb, did assist the Muslim army in their suppression of the rebellion of Mahra.

Notwithstanding Hamdān didn't have own statehood and was an ally or a vassal of Ḥimyar, it was mentioned frequently in Sabaic inscriptions. The main event in which Hamdān took part was the siege of Naǧrān, and they seem to have converted to Judaism prior to Islam, at least partially. This tribe wasn't mentioned in the medieval sources either as rebels or as allies, apart from an unidentified number of Hamdānids which took part in the death of al-ʾAswad al-ʿAnsī, which indicates that the tribe as a whole probably remained loyal to the Islamic state and that their political power remained relatively unchanged compared to the pre-Islamic period.

Ḫawlan was the name shared by two tribes, the northern and the southern Ḫawlan. They were primarily portrayed as the vassals of Ḥimyar and took part in the Ḥimyarite conquest of South Arabia as their vassals. Ḫawlan is mentioned in the account of the Wars of apostasy only once, as a place where the one of the appointed governors of the Muslim state over Yemen sought refuge after the rebellion broke out.

Ḥimyar's role in ancient South Arabia was crucial: this tribe managed to fully unify South Arabia for the first time in history, and they managed to unify it not only politically but culturally as well, by imposing Sabaic language and by later conversion to monotheism. This kingdom, and all of South Arabia with it, lost its independence, first to Ethiopia and then to Sassanid Persia. Compared to how often the name of Ḥimyar is mentioned in the pre-Islamic South Arabian inscriptions, the fact the it's mentioned so rarely in the a aṭ-Ṭabarī's history, and the fact that they appear to have remained loyal to the Islamic state throughout the Wars of apostasy, seems to indicate that Ḥimyar had lost the dominant role it had enjoyed in pre-Islamic South Arabia.

Kinda was an important tribe in pre-Islamic South Arabia, since they achieved control of central Arabia, although it never managed to gain independence from the dominant powers of the era, being vassals of Ḥimyar first and then Ethiopia. They suffered a reversal of fortune, however, as they rebelled against the Islamic state and were severaly defeated by the Muslim army.

Maḏḥiǧ is mentioned in a small number of inscriptions, but that small number indicates that they could not have been an influential polity in ancient South Arabia. They were the first to rebel under the leadership of al-ʾAswad al-ʿAnsī, but were reincorporated into the Caliphate after his death.

The tribe of Murād, which is a part of the tribal group of Maḏḥiǧ, is mentioned in an even smaller number of inscriptions, but their political role is clear: they were vassals of ʾAbraha, the Aksumite king of Ḥimyar. During the events after the death of the prophet Muḥammad, this tribe did not take part in either the rebellion or in its suppression. A member of this tribe, Qays b. ʿAbd Yaġūṯ al-Murādī, was influential however; he was a general of al-

ʾAswad al-ʿAnsī who killed him and led the rebellion himself afterward. Another important member of tribe of Murād was ʿAbd al-Rahman ibn Mulǧam al-Murādī, a Ḫāriǧī who killed the fourth caliph ʿAlī bin Abī Ṭālib.[311]

Mahra is mentioned in a small number of inscriptions, and they don't seem to have taken part in any of the major events in ancient South Arabian history. They did rebel against the Caliphate, however, but due to their discord they were defeated and joined the Muslim army in the suppression of the rebellion of other tribes.

CONCLUSION

South Arabia experienced important political and cultural transformation with the arrival of Islam. The transitional period between ancient South Arabia and Islamic Yemen can be seen as decline and break with the past, or as a transitional period. Political transformation, which was the result of acceptance of Islam, influenced the relations between South Arabian tribes on a political level.

The majority of research focuses either on history of individual tribes or on the political processes as a whole; therefore there is a gap in research at the intermediate level. This intermediate level can be researched by investigating the relations between the tribes. The time focus of research is mostly either on the period before or the period after Islamization.

The political situation in ancient South Arabia before the rise of Islam was characterized by both a tendency of political unification as well as division. Division was the

311 EI^3, s.v. Ibn Muljam (L. Veccia Vaglieri)

dominant trend. Despite the struggle of ancient kingdoms for dominance over South Arabia and final unification of the entire region under Ḥimyar, fragmentation was the dominant factor in tribal relations. Tribal relations were dynamic, alternating between alliances and conflicts. Ultimately, political instability and fragmentation became the factors of decline of ancient South Arabian civilization. Attempts to unite the region by administrative measures, and the use of monotheism to achieve political consolidation, proved to be unsuccessfu. The influence of Judaism and Christianity only increased the level of fragmentation and made the relations between various political forces more difficult.

Conversion to Islam and the subsequent events, especially the Ridda Wars, brought about important changes in inter-tribal relations and the division of power in the region. Political alliance with the Caliphate or struggle against it gave various tribes a chance to change their political status. Event though these changes didn't affect those tribes which were politically insignificant. However, the important tribes mostly lost their dominant role in the region. Some of them led the rebellion, while others immediately took the side of the caliphate, whereas others were too insignificant to play an important role one way or the other. Unlike Judaism and Christianity, the conversion to Islam did prove to be a successful unifying factor for South Arabia, since the region remains a part of the Islamic civilization to this day.

BIBLIOGRAPHY:

Primary sources:

1. Corpus of South Arabian Inscriptions. DASI: Digital Archive for the Study of pre-islamic Arabian Inscriptions [http://dasi.humnet.unipi.it].

2. Al-Ṭabarī, Abū Ǧaʿfar Muḥammad ibn Jarīr: *Tārīḫ al-Umam wa-l-Mulūk (History of the Prophets and Kings)*, ed. Abū Ṣahīb al-Karmī. Bayt al-Afkār ad-Duwaliyya.

3. The History of al- Ṭabarī. Volume X. The Conquest of Arabia, trans. Fred M. Donner. Albany: State University of New York Press, 1993.

Secondary sources:

1. Arbach, Mounir and Rossi, Irene: "From city-state to kingdom: history and chronology of Ma'īn between the VIII and the VI centuries BC. " *Orientalia*, 81/4 (2012), pp. 318-339.
2. Al-Asali, Khalid Salih: *South Arabia in the 5th and 6th centuries CE, with reference to relations with Central Arabia*. Ph.D. Diss., University of St. Andrews, 1968.
3. van Alfen, Peter: "Die Studies of the Earliest Qatabanian and Sabaean Coinages." *Coinage of the Caravan Kingdoms: Studies in the Monetization of Ancient Arabia*. Eds. M. Huth and P. van Alfen. New York: American Numismatic Society, 2010 (Numismatic Studies 25), pp. 257- 302.
4. Bāfaqīh, Muḥammad 'Abd al-Qādir: L'unification du Yémen antique: la lutte entre Saba, Himyar et le Hadramawt du 1er au IIIème siècle de l'ère chrétienne. Paris: Librairie OrientalistPaul Geuthner, 1990 (Bibliotheque de Raydan, 1).
5. Beeston, A.F.L: "Kingship in Ancient South Arabia." *Journal of the Economic and Social History of the Orient*, Vol. 15, No. 3 (1972), pp. 256-268.
6. Beeston, A.F.L: "Languages of pre-Islamic Arabia." *Arabica*, Vol. 28, Issue 2 (1981), pp. 178-186.
7. Beeston, A. F. L.: "Some Features of Social Structure in Saba. *Studies in the History of Arabia. Vol. I. Sources for the History of Arabia*. Ed. A.M. Abdallah, et al. Riyadh: University of Riyadh, 1979, pp. 115–23.
8. Beeston, A.F.L: "The Arabian Aromatics Trade in Antiquity." *Proceedings of the Seminar for Arabian Studies*, 2005, pp. 53-64.

9. Beeston, A.F.L: "The Religions of Pre-Islamic Yemen." L'Arabie du Sud. Histoire et Civilisation, vol. I:Le peuple Yemenite et ses raciness. Ed. J. Chelhod. Paris, 1984 (Islam d'hier et d'aujourd'hui, 21), pp. 267–268.
10. Bron, François: "La crise du royaume de Saba' au II ème siècle de notre ère." *Orientalia* NOVA SERIES, Vol. 71, No. 4 (2002), pp. 417-423.
11. Bukharin, Mikhail: "Towards the earliest history of Kinda." *Arabian Archaeology and Epigraphy*, 20 (2009), pp. 64–80.
12. Drewes, A.J, et al, "Some absolute dates for the development of the South Arabian script", in Arabian Archaeology and Epigraphy, 24, (2013), 205-206.
13. Francuzov, Sergej: *Istorija Hadramauta s drevnejshih vremen do konca britanskogo vladychestva. Tom 1. Istorija Hadramauta v epohu drevnosti* [History of Hadramaut from ancient times to the end of British rule. Volume 1. History of Hadramaut in the Age of Antiquity]. Sankt-Peterburg: Peterburgskoe lingvisticheskoe obshhestvo, 2014 (Studia Yemenica).
14. Gajda, Iwona: *Le royaume de Himyar à l'époque monothéiste.* Paris: De Boccard, 2009 (Mémoires de l'Académie des inscriptions et belles-lettres, 40).
15. Hoyland, Robert G*: Arabia and the Arabs, From the Bronze Age to the Coming of Islam*. New York: Routledge, 2001.
16. Huth, Martin: "Athenian Imitations from Arabia." *Coinage of the Caravan Kingdoms: Studies in the Monetization of Ancient Arabia*. Eds. M. Huth. P. van Alfen. New York: American Numismatic Society, 2010 (Numismatic Studies 25), pp. 227-256.
17. Huth, Martin and Peter G. van Alfen: "Introduction." *Coinage of the Caravan Kingdoms: Studies in the Monetization of Ancient Arabia*. Eds. M. Huth and P. van Alfen. New York: American Numismatic Society, 2010 (Numismatic Studies 25), pp. 1-25.
18. Kogan, Leonid and Andrey Korotayev: "Sayhadic Languages (Epigraphic South Arabian). " *Semitic Languages*. Ed. Robert Hetzron. London: Routledge, 1997, pp. 220-242.

19. Kościelniak, Krzysztof: "Jewish and Christian religious influences on pre-Islamic Arabia on the example of the term RḤMNN ("the Merciful")." *Orientalia Christiana Cracoviensia*, 3 (2011), pp. 67-74.
20. Korotayev, Andrey: "A socio-political conflict in the Qatabanian kingdom? (A preliminary re-interpretation of the Qatabanic inscription RÉS 3566)." *Proceedings of the Seminar for Arabian Studies,* Vol. 27 (1997), pp. 141-158.
21. Korotayev, Andrey: "Internal Structure of Middle Sabaean Bayt." *Arabian Archaeology and Epigraphy*, 5 (1994), pp. 174–183.
22. Korotayev, Andrey: *Pre-Islamic Yemen.* Wiesbaden: Harrassowitz Verlag, 1996.
23. Korotayev, Andrey: *Social'naja istorija Jemena, X v. do n.e. - XX v. n.e. Vozhdestva i plemena strany Hashid i Bakil* [Social History of Yemen, X century. BCE - XX century CE. The Chiefdoms and Tribes of the Country Hashid and Bakil]. Moskva: URSS, 2006.
24. Lecker, Michael: "Judaism among Kinda and the Ridda of Kinda." *Journal of the American Oriental Society*, Vol. 115, No. 4 (1995), pp. 635-650.
25. Lundin, Avraam: *Juzhnaja Aravija v VI veke* [South Arabia in the 6th Century]. Moskva, Leningrad: Izdatel'stvo Akademii nauk SSSR, 1961 (Palestinskij sbornik 8(71)).
26. Lundin, Avraam: *Gosudarstvo mukarribov Saba : sabejskij eponimat* [The State of Mukarribs - Saba: Sabean eponymat]. Moskva: Nauka, 171.
27. Lundin, Avraam: "Prestolonasledie v Katabane" [Succession in Qatabān]. *Sovetskaja etnografija*, 4 (1978), pp. 123-130.
28. Al-Medej, A A M M M: *Yemeni relations with the central Islamic authorities: (9-233/630-847); a political history*. Ph.D. Diss., Durham University, 1983.
29. Maraqten, Mohammed: "Writing Materials in pre-Islamic Arabia." *Journal of Semitic Studies* XLIII/2 (1998), pp. 287-310.
30. Nebes, Norbert: "Die Märtyrer von Nagrān und das Ende der Ḥimyar. Zur politischen Geschichte Südarabiens im frühen sechsten Jahrhundert." *Aethiopica*, 11 (2021), pp. 7-40.

31. Piotrovsky, Mikhail: *Juzhnaja Aravija v rannee srednevekov'e. Stanovlenie srednevekovogo obshhestva* [South Arabia in the Early Middle Ages. The Formation of a Medieval Society]. Moskva: Nauka, 1985.
32. Pirenne, Jacqueline*: Le royaume sud-arabe de Qataban et sa datation: d'apres l'archeologie et les sources classiques jusqu'au Periple de la Mer Erythree.* Louvain: Publications universitaires, 1961.
33. Pirenne, Jacqueline: *Paléographie des inscriptions sud-arabes. Contribution à la chronologie et à l'histoire de l'Arabie du Sud antique, Tome I: Des origines jusqu'à l'époque himyarite*. Bruxelles: Paleis der Academiën, 1956 (Verhandelingen van de Koninklijke Vlaamse Academie voor Wetenschappen, Letteren en Schone Kunsten van België. Klasse der Letteren, 26).
34. Prioletta, Alessia: "A new monotheistic inscription from the Military Museum of Ṣanʿā." In *New research in archaeology and epigraphy of South Arabia and its neighbors*. Proceedings of the "Rencontres Sabéennes 15" held in Moscow, May 25th –27th, 2011. Ed. by A.V. Sedov. Moscow: The State Museum of Oriental Art, 2012, pp. 315-332.
35. Ryckmans, Jacques: *L'Institution monarchique en Arabie méridionale avant l'Islam: Maʿîn et Saba.* Louvain: Publications universitaires, 1951.
36. Robin, Christian: "Arabia and Ethiopia." *The Oxford Handbook of late Antiquity*. Ed. Scott Fitzgerald Johnson. New York: Oxford University Press, 2012, pp. 247-335.
37. Robin, Christian: "Aux Origines de l'État Himyarite: Ḥimyar et Dhu-Raydan." *Arabian Studies in Honour of Mahmoud Ghul.* Wiesbaden: Harrassowitz Verlag, 1989, pp. 104–112.
38. Robin, Christian: "Before Himyar: Epigraphic Evidence for the Kingdoms of South Arabia." *Arabs and Empires before Islam.* Ed. Greg Fisher. New York: Oxford University Press, 2015, pp. 90-127.
39. Robin, Christian: "Du paganisme au monothéisme." *Revue du monde musulman et de la Méditerranée*, 61 (1991), pp. 139-155.
40. Robin, Christian: "Esquisse d'une histoire de l'organisation tribale en Arabie du Sud antique." *La péninsule Arabique d'aujourd'hui.* T. II. *Etudes par pays.* Éd. P.

Bonnenfant. Aix-en-Provence: Institut de recherches et d'études sur le monde arabe et musulman, 1982, pp. 17–30.

41. Robin, Christian: "Himyarite kings on coinage." *Coinage of the Caravan Kingdoms: Studies in the Monetization of Ancient Arabia*. Eds. M. Huth. P. van Alfen. New York: American Numismatic Society, 2010 (Numismatic Studies 25), pp.357-383.
42. Robin, Christian: "La pénétration des Arabes nomades au Yémen." *Revue du monde musulman et de la Méditerranée*, Vol. 61, N. 1 (1991), pp. 71-88.
43. Robin, Christian: "Le judaïsme de Ḥimyar." *Arabia*, 1 (2003), pp. 97-172.
44. Robin, Christian: *Le pays de Ḥamdān et Ḥawlān Quḍāʿat (Nord-Yemen), avant l'Islam.* Diss., Paris, 1977.
45. Robin, Christian: "Le problème de Hamdān: des qayls aux trois tribus." *Proceedings of the Seminar for Arabian Studies,* Vol. 8 (1978), pp. 46-52.
46. Robin, Christian: "Le royaume hujride, dit « royaume de Kinda », entre Himyar et Byzance." *Comptes rendus des séances de l'Académie des Inscriptions et Belles-Lettres*, Vol. 140, N. 2 (1996), pp. 665-714.
47. Robin, Christian: "Les inscriptions de l'arabie antique et les études arabes." *Arabica,48* / 4 (2001), pp. 509-577.
48. Robin, Christian: " Les langues de la Péninsule Arabique." *Revue du monde musulman et de la Méditerranée*, Vol. 61, N. 1 (1991), pp. 89-111.
49. Robin, Christian: "Les religions pratiquées par les membres de la tribu de Kinda (Arabie) à la veille de l'Islam." *Judaism ancien - Ancient Judaism*, 1 (2013), pp.203-261.
50. Robin, Christian: "Les rois de Kinda." *Arabia, Greece and Byzantium. Cultural Contacts in Ancient and Medieval Times*. Eds. by Abdulaziz Al-Helabi [et al.]. Riyadh: King Saud University, Department of History, 2012, pp. 59-129.
51. Robin, Christian: "Nagrān vers l'époque du massacre: notes sur l'histoire politique, économique et institutionnelle et sur l'introduction du christianisme." *Juifs et chrétiens en Arabie aux Ve et VIe siècles: regards croisés sur les sources.* Éd. J. Beaucamp, F. Briquel-Chatonnet et Ch.Robin. Paris: ACHCByz, 2010 (Monographies 32 - Le massacre de Nagrān II), pp. 39-106.

52. Robin, Christian: "Saba' et la Khawlān du Nord (Khawlān Gudādān): l'organisation et la gestion des conquêtes par les royaumes d'Arabie méridionale." *Issledovanija po Aravii i islamu. Sbornik statej b čect' 70-letija Muhaila Borisoviča Piotrovskogo* [Studies on Arabia and Islam. A collection of papers in honour of Mikhail Borishovich Piotrovskij on the occasion of his 70th birthday]. Ed. Alexander V. Sedov. Moskva: Gosudarstvennyj Muzej Vostoka, 2014, pp. 156-203.
53. Robin, Christian: "Quelques épisodes marquants de l'histoire sudarabique." *Revue du monde musulman et de la Méditerranée*, Vol. 61, N. 1 (1991), pp. 55-70.
54. Sedov, Alexander: "Sea-trade of the Hadramawt Kingdom from the 1st to the 6th Centuries A.D." *Profumi d'Arabia. Atti del convegno.* A cura di A.Avanzini. Roma: L'Erma di Bretschneider, 1997 (Saggi di storia antica, 11), pp. 365-385.
55. Schiettecatte, Jérémie: "À la veille de l'"islam: effondrement ou transformation du monde antique." *Les préludes de l'islam. Ruptures et continuités des civilisations du Proche-Orient, de l'Afrique orientale, de l'Arabie et de l'Inde à la veille de l'Islam.* Éd. Christian Robin et Jérémie Schiettecatte. Paris: De Boccard, 2013 (Orient et Méditerranée, 11), pp. 9-36.
56. Schiettecatte, Jérémie: "L'évolution du peuplement sudarabique du Ier au VIe siècle." *L'Arabie à la veille de l'islam. Un bilan clinique.* Éd. Christian Robin et Jérémie Schiettecatte. Paris: Diffusion De Boccard, 2008 (Orient et Méditerranée, 3), pp. 217-249.
57. Schiettecatte, Jérémie: "Ports et commerce maritime dans l'"Arabie du Sud préislamique." *Chroniques yéménites*, 15 (2008), pp. 65-90.
58. Shoufani, Elias: *Al-Riddah and the Muslim conquest of Arabia.* Toronto: University of Toronto Press, 1973.
59. Stein, Peter: " Palaeography of the Ancient South Arabian script. New evidence for an absolute chronology." *Arabian Archaeol Epigraphy*, 24 (2013), pp. 186–195.
60. Stein, Peter: "The 'Ḥimyaritic' Language in preislamic Yemen – A Critical Re-evaluation." *Semitica et Classica*, 1 (2008), pp. 203-212.
61. Stein, Peter: "Zur Dialektgeographie des Sabäischen." *Journal of Semitic Studies*, 49/2 (2004), pp. 225-245.

62. Al-Zahrani, Mahfouz Said: *L'histoire des tribus Kinda et Madhhij en Arabie preislamique, des origines jusqu'au VIe siecle de l'ere chretienne*. Thesis, Aix-en-Provence: Université de Provence, 2000.

Appendix

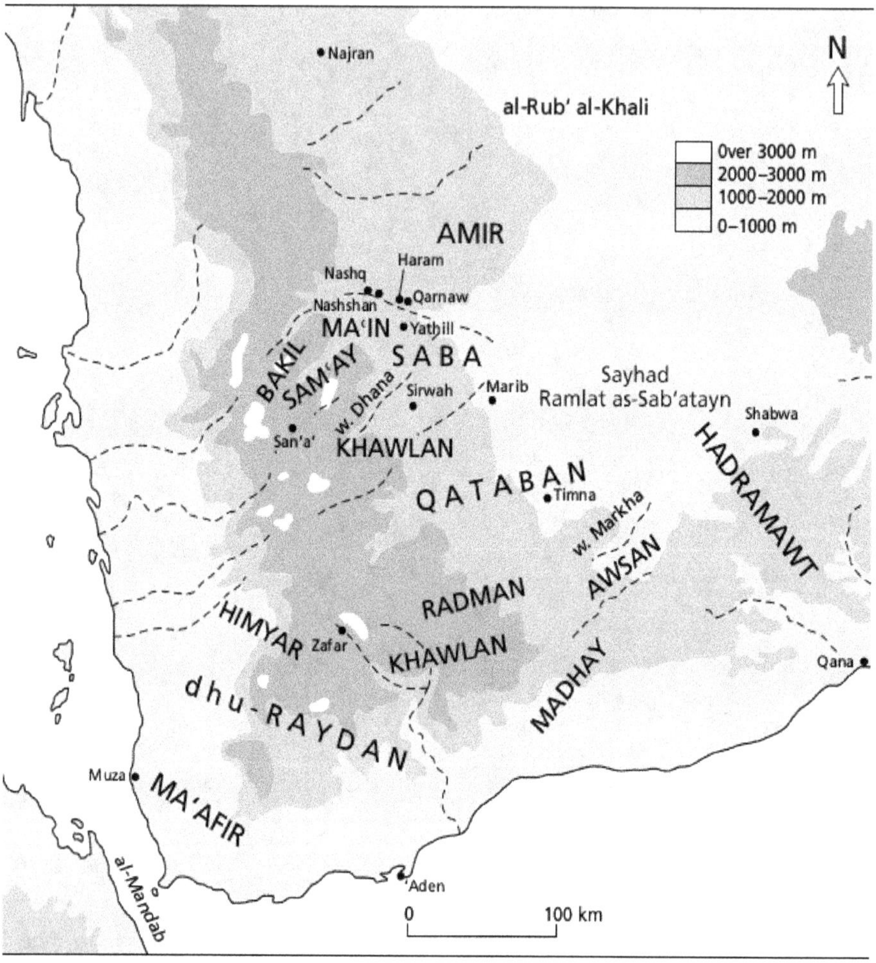

Figure 1. Map of South Arabia (adapted by author from Christian Robin, 'La Fin du royaume de Ma'in', 179).

Source: Robert G. Hoyland*: Arabia and the Arabs, From the Bronze Age to the Coming of Islam*. New York: Routledge, 2001, p. 37.

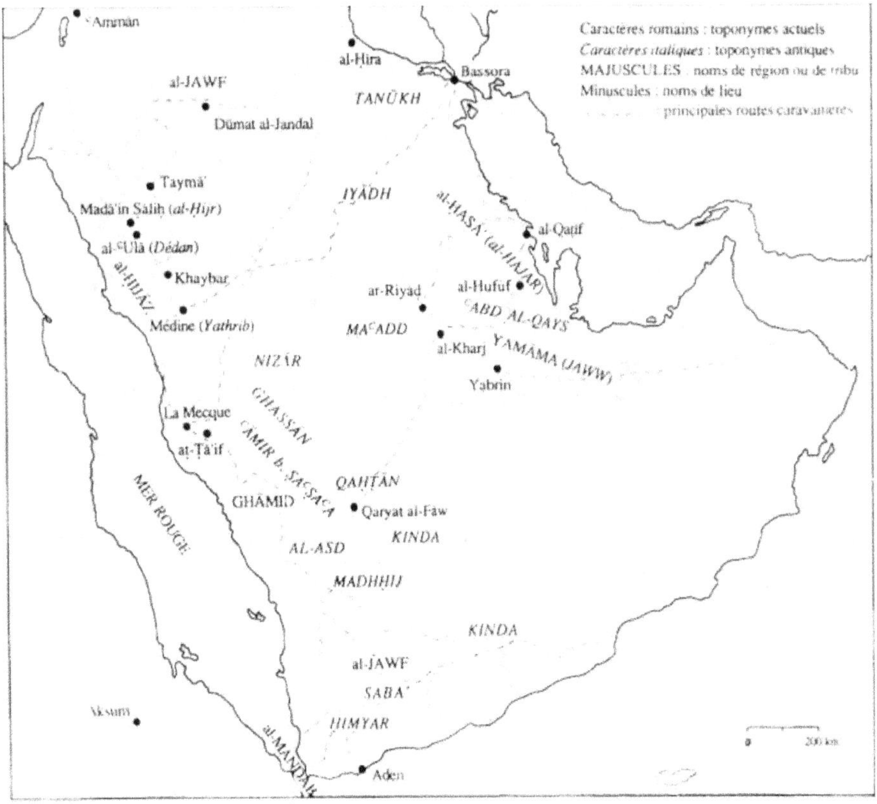

Figure 2. The Arabian Peninsula

Source: Christian Robin: " Introduction." *Revue du monde musulman et de la Méditerranée*, Vol. 61, N. 1 (1991), p. 12.

Figure 3. The inscription CIH 325.

Source: Corpus of South Arabian Inscriptions. DASI: Digital Archive for the Study of pre-islamic Arabian Inscriptions [http://dasi.humnet.unipi.it].

Figure 4. The inscription CIH 541.

Source: Corpus of South Arabian Inscriptions. DASI: Digital Archive for the Study of pre-islamic Arabian Inscriptions [http://dasi.humnet.unipi.it].

Abstract

The purpose of this Master's Thesis is to analyze the cultural and political changes which the tribes which populated South Arabia underwent during the transitional period from the 6th century CE to the conquest and inclusion of South Arabia into the Islamic caliphate. South Arabia had, prior to the Islamic conquest, constituted a distinct civilization, with its own social structure, languages, script, religion, and identity. After the inclusion of this region into the Islamic caliphate, South Arabia became a part of the Arabic and Islamic civilization.

This thesis investigates how the political situation of South Arabian tribes changed due to the adoption of Islam. The main goal behind this thesis is to compare the historical sources regarding ancient South Arabian tribes. The thesis is therefore methodologically based on a comparative analysis of tribal organization and power relations between ancient South Arabian tribes. This comparative analysis includes the juxtaposition of historical sources, both the pre-Islamic South Arabian inscriptions as well as the later Islamic medieval historiography.

Zusammenfassung

Der Zweck dieser Masterarbeit ist es, die kulturellen und politischen Veränderungen zu analysieren, die die Stämme, die Südarabien besiedelten, während der Übergangszeit vom 6. Jahrhundert bis zur Eroberung und Einbeziehung von Südarabien in das islamische Kalifat unterzogen wurden. Südarabien hatte vor der islamischen Eroberung eine eigene Zivilisation mit eigener Gesellschaftsstruktur, Sprachen, Schrift, Religion und Identität. Südarabien wurde, nach der Integration dieser Region in das islamische Kalifat, ein Teil der arabischen und islamischen Zivilisation.

Diese These untersucht, wie sich die politische Situation der südarabischen Stämme aufgrund ihrer Annahme des Islams verändert hat. Das Hauptziel dieser These ist es, die historischen Quellen über alte südarabischen Stämme zu vergleichen. Die These basiert methodologisch auf der vergleichenden Analyse der Stammesorganisation und der Machtbeziehungen zwischen alten südarabischen Stämmen. Diese vergleichende Analyse beinhaltet Vergleich der historischen Quellen, sowohl der vorislamischen südarabischen Inschriften als auch der späteren islamischen mittelalterlichen Geschichtsschreibung.

www.ingramcontent.com/pod-product-compliance
Lightning Source LLC
LaVergne TN
LVHW020427080526
838202LV00055B/5057
* 9 7 8 5 2 0 5 2 1 4 7 8 0 *